Careers in Focus

CONSTRUCTION

FIFTH EDITION

Ferguson
An imprint of Infobase Publishing

Careers in Focus: Construction, Fifth Edition

Ferguson
An imprint of Infobase Publishing
132 West 31st Street
New York NY 10001

Library of Congress Cataloging-in-Publication Data

Careers in focus. Construction. — 5th ed.
    p. cm. — (Careers in focus)
  Includes bibliographical references and index.
  ISBN-13: 978-0-8160-8018-2 (hardcover : alk. paper)
  ISBN-10: 0-8160-8018-6 (hardcover : alk. paper) 1. Building trades—Vocational guidance—Juvenile literature. I. Ferguson Publishing. II. Title: Construction.
  TH159.C37 2010
  690.023—dc22
                                         2009045513

Ferguson books are available at special discounts when purchased in bulk quantities for businesses, associations, institutions, or sales promotions. Please call our Special Sales Department in New York at (212) 967-8800 or (800) 322-8755.

You can find Ferguson on the World Wide Web at http://www.fergpubco.com

Text design by David Strelecky
Composition by Mary Susan Ryan-Flynn
Cover printed by Art Print, Taylor, PA
Book printed and bound by Maple Press, York, PA
Date printed: April 2010
Printed in the United States of America

10 9 8 7 6 5 4 3 2 1

This book is printed on acid-free paper.

All links and Web addresses were checked and verified to be correct at the time of publication. Because of the dynamic nature of the Web, some addresses and links may have changed since publication and may no longer be valid.

Table of Contents

Introduction

Construction is a complex industry dealing with all aspects of building structures, from skyscrapers to highways. Construction work includes both clearing sites and developing structures. Construction also covers integral structural service equipment, such as plumbing, heating, central air-conditioning, electrical wiring, lighting equipment, elevators, and escalators.

In general, the first step in construction involves bidding for a project. The contractor who bids the lowest price is not always awarded the contract. Bids are judged on several points: experience of the contractor, designs submitted for the project, proposed time schedule, recommendations from previous customers, and cost. The winning contractor then hires subcontractors to perform selected projects, such as laying the foundation, fireproofing the structure, and installing the ventilation system. After all of the tasks have been coordinated with the subcontractors, the construction is ready to begin.

Construction takes many forms, and its projects vary widely in size, appearance, composition, character, and purpose. These projects are divided into major groups or categories according to their principal characteristics, and each of these is further divided into subcategories. The categories apply to new construction as well as repair and renovation work.

One group includes structures ranging from small homes to huge housing developments; these are part of what is called residential building construction.

Another major category is nonresidential building construction, or general building construction. It includes industrial buildings, such as plants and factories; commercial structures, ranging from small stores to great skyscrapers; and institutional and other kinds of nonresidential structures, such as schools, churches and other religious structures, and hospitals.

Highway and heavy construction is another principal category. Highway work embraces not only networks of interstate highways, but also bridges, local roads, and streets. Airport runway construction is largely done by highway contractors, since building runways and highways involves much the same methods, materials, machines, and skills. Typical heavy projects include dams, big bridges, tunnels, railroads, missile bases, refineries, and waterways such as the Panama Canal, the St. Lawrence Seaway, and river channels. Similar equipment and construction methods are employed for highway and heavy construction. Earthmoving, for example, may be done for a highway project or for an earth-fill dam.

Finally, municipal utilities construction encompasses the essential services for counties, towns, and cities. Such projects include sewage treatment plants, water purification projects, water and sewer lines, underground utilities, street resurfacing, park and playground construction, and sidewalk construction and maintenance.

Construction activity is divided into two broad classifications: private and public. Private construction is work performed for private owners, whether individuals, corporations, or other business firms, organizations, or institutions of a nongovernmental character. It is usually paid for out of private funds. Public construction is construction work performed for federal, state, or local agencies of government and usually paid for out of tax money, bonds, or other public funds. However, the governing distinction between private and public construction is the ownership of the project at the time of construction and not the source of funds used to pay for the project.

For most of the trades involved in construction, the workers do not start at the beginning of the building process and work until the building is complete. Workers come in for their portion of the job and then move on to other projects. So an electrician comes in to wire a house and then moves on to another construction site. He or she may have to come back to do more electrical work, but it is not essential to have an electrician at a job site every day. Because workers come and go, it is important to have a project supervisor, or job foreman, or a construction manager, who knows all the phases of the work being done.

Construction accounts for approximately one-tenth of the U.S. annual gross national product. The largest areas on which individuals and businesses spend money are physical facilities: homes, stores and buildings, mills and factories, highways and streets, bridges, railroads, airports, wharves and docks, pipelines, tunnels, dams, power plants, irrigation projects, public works, and defense installations.

Whether it is the life savings of one family buying a home, or the investments of an insurance company to finance the erection of a skyscraper for a corporation, it all adds up to a substantial yearly increase in national investment. The nation's banks, insurance companies, pension plans, and other financial institutions have a big stake in construction, for they finance most of it.

The nation is continually forced to make major repairs to its infrastructure—highways, tunnels, bridges, dams, schools, power plants, water and sewer systems, subways, airports—which ensures the need for all kinds of employment in highway and heavy construction work.

In addition to the increased numbers of projects, the projects themselves will grow in both size and complexity in coming years. New laws setting higher standards for building and construction materials, worker safety, energy efficiency, and pollution control will need to be addressed by skilled professionals with expertise in construction science, engineering, and management. Employment of construction managers, who oversee projects and ensure that laws dealing with construction, safety, and the environment are upheld, is expected to grow faster than the average for all careers through 2016. Managers with a bachelor's degree in construction science and work experience in construction management services firms should have plenty of job opportunities.

The continuing need for new homes, commercial and office buildings, and factories, plus the repair and maintenance of these and other structures, will create additional jobs in the residential and nonresidential building categories.

Job growth also will occur in most of the skilled construction trades, especially for electricians. They will be needed in greater numbers not only to replace old wiring in existing facilities but to keep pace with the continuing growth in telecommunications and computer equipment now used in many new structures, including electronically operated "smart" buildings. Opportunities will also be available for electricians who specialize in renewable energy technology.

All these factors point to a steady expansion of the market for construction services. Although further technological improvements in construction methods and equipment may be expected to raise the productivity of workers, the volume of activity will require substantial numbers of craft workers in the various building trades, mostly as replacements for those who retire or leave the labor force for other reasons.

One major trend in the industry is the emergence of green construction practices. These are defined by the U.S. Environmental Protection Agency as the "practice of creating structures and using processes that are environmentally responsible and resource-efficient throughout a building's life-cycle from siting to design, construction, operation, maintenance, renovation, and deconstruction." The number of green construction jobs is expected to grow significantly in coming years.

Although prospects look promising, the construction industry is very sensitive to fluctuations in the national economy. These fluctuations usually affect part-time and seasonal workers and less-skilled workers the most. However, skilled tradespeople are almost always in demand, even during economic downturns. Opportunities are expected to be strongest in nonresidential construction, including heavy and civil engineering construction (the construction and repair of highways, bridges, and streets).

The articles in *Careers in Focus: Construction* appear in Ferguson's *Encyclopedia of Careers and Vocational Guidance,* but have been updated and revised with the latest information from the U.S. Department of Labor, professional organizations, and other sources.

The following paragraphs detail the sections and features that appear in the book.

The **Quick Facts** section provides a brief summary of the career, including recommended school subjects, personal skills, work environment, minimum educational requirements, salary ranges, certification or licensing requirements, and employment outlook. This section also provides acronyms and identification numbers for the following government classification indexes: the Dictionary of Occupational Titles (DOT), the Guide for Occupational Exploration (GOE), the National Occupational Classification (NOC) Index, and the Occupational Information Network (O*NET)-Standard Occupational Classification System (SOC) index. The DOT, GOE, and O*NET-SOC indexes have been created by the U.S. government; the NOC index is Canada's career-classification system. Readers can use the identification numbers listed in the Quick Facts section to access further information about a career. Print editions of the DOT (*Dictionary of Occupational Titles.* Indianapolis, Ind.: JIST Works, 1991) and GOE (*Guide for Occupational Exploration.* Indianapolis, Ind.: JIST Works, 2001) are available at libraries. Electronic versions of the NOC (http:// http://www5.hrsdc.gc.ca/NOC/) and O*NET-SOC (http://online.onetcenter.org) are available on the Internet. When no DOT, GOE, NOC, or O*NET-SOC numbers are present, this means that the U.S. Department of Labor or Human Resources Development Canada have not created a numerical designation for this career. In this instance, you will see the acronym "N/A," or not available.

The **Overview** section is a brief introductory description of the duties and responsibilities involved in this career. Oftentimes, a career may have a variety of job titles. When this is the case, alternative career titles are presented. Employment statistics are also provided, when available. The **History** section describes the history of the particular job as it relates to the overall development of its industry or field. **The Job** describes the primary and secondary duties of the job. **Requirements** discusses high school and postsecondary education and training requirements, any certification or licensing that is necessary, and other personal requirements for success in the job. **Exploring** offers suggestions on how to gain experience in or knowledge of the particular job before making a firm educational and financial commitment. The focus is on what can be done while still in high school (or in the early years of college) to gain a better understanding of the job. The **Employers** section gives an overview of typical places of employment for the job. **Starting Out** discusses the best ways to land that first job, be it through the college career services office, newspaper ads, Internet employment sites, or personal contact. The **Advancement** section describes what kind of career path to expect from the job and how to get there. **Earnings** lists salary ranges and describes the typical fringe benefits. The **Work Environment** section describes the typical surroundings and conditions of employment—whether indoors or outdoors, noisy or quiet, social or independent. Also discussed are typical hours worked, any seasonal fluctuations, and the stresses and strains of the job. The **Outlook** section summarizes the job in terms of the general economy and industry projections. For the most part, Outlook information is obtained from the U.S. Bureau of Labor Statistics and is supplemented by information gathered from professional associations. Job growth terms follow those used in the *Occupational Outlook Handbook*. Growth described as "much faster than the average" means an increase of 21 percent or more. Growth described as "faster than the average" means an increase of 14 to 20 percent. Growth described as "about as fast as the average" means an increase of 7 to 13 percent. Growth described as "more slowly than the average" means an increase of 3 to 6 percent. "Little or no change" means a decrease of 2 percent to an increase of 2 percent. "Decline" means a decrease of 3 percent or more. Each article ends with **For More Information,** which lists organizations that provide information on training, education, internships, scholarships, and job placement.

Careers in Focus: Construction also includes photos, sidebars, and interviews with professionals in the field.

A career in construction is challenging on many fronts, as the work can involve outdoor physical labor in all kinds of weather, detailed strategizing and negotiating with workers and clients, and irregular work schedules. However, people involved in construction can also look at the end result of their work and know that they had a direct hand in creating something that will be enjoyed and used by people for years to come. Few professions offer this type of satisfaction. If you are interested in a future in construction, take the time to read about the many different careers described in this book and contact the organizations listed for more information.

Architects

OVERVIEW

Architects plan, design, and observe construction of facilities used for human occupancy and of other structures. They consult with clients, plan layouts of buildings, prepare drawings of proposed buildings, write specifications, and prepare scale and full-sized drawings. Architects also may help clients obtain bids, select a contractor, and negotiate the construction contract, and they also visit construction sites to ensure that the work is being completed according to specification. There are approximately 141,200 architects working in the United States.

HISTORY

Architecture began not with shelters for people to live in but with the building of religious structures—from Stonehenge in England and the pyramids in Egypt to pagodas in Japan and the Parthenon in Greece. It was the Romans who developed a new building method—concrete vaulting—that made possible large cities with permanent masonry buildings. As they extended the Roman Empire, they built for public and military purposes. They developed and built apartment buildings, law courts, public baths, theaters, and circuses. The industrial revolution with its demand for factories and mills developed iron and steel construction, which evolved into the steel and glass skyscraper of today.

The history of architecture follows that of human civilization, so the architecture of any period reflects the culture of that time and place. Architecture of early periods has influenced that of later centuries, including the work of contemporary architects. The field

QUICK FACTS

School Subjects
Art
Mathematics

Personal Skills
Artistic
Communication/ideas

Work Environment
Primarily indoors
Primarily one location

Minimum Education Level
Bachelor's degree

Salary Range
$41,320 to $70,320 to
$119,220

Certification or Licensing
Voluntary (certification)
Required (licensing)

Outlook
Faster than the average

DOT
001

GOE
02.07.03

NOC
2151

O*NET-SOC
17-1011.00

continues to develop as new techniques and materials are discovered and as architects blend creativity with function.

THE JOB

The architect normally has two responsibilities: to design a building that will satisfy the client and to protect the public's health, safety, and welfare. This second responsibility requires architects to be licensed by the state in which they work. Meeting the first responsibility involves many steps. The job begins with learning what the client wants. The architect takes many factors into consideration, including local and state building and design regulations, climate, soil on which the building is to be constructed, zoning laws, fire regulations, and the client's financial limitations.

The architect then prepares a set of plans that, upon the client's approval, will be developed into final design and construction documents. These plans are typically created using computer-aided design and drafting or building information modeling technology, although some architects still draw their designs by hand. The final design shows the exact dimensions of every portion of the building, including the location and size of columns and beams, electrical outlets and fixtures, plumbing, heating and air-conditioning facilities, windows, and doors. The architect works closely with consulting engineers on the specifics of the plumbing, heating, air-conditioning, and electrical work to be done.

The architect then assists the client in getting bids from general contractors, one of whom will be selected to construct the building to the specifications. The architect helps the client through the completion of the construction and occupancy phases, making certain the correct materials are used and that the drawings and specifications are faithfully followed.

Throughout the process the architect works closely with a design or project team. This team is usually made up of the following: *designers,* who specialize in design development; a *structural designer,* who designs the frame of the building in accordance with the work of the architect; the *project manager* or *job superintendent,* who sees that the full detail drawings are completed to the satisfaction of the architect; and the *specification writer* and *estimator,* who prepare a project manual that describes in more detail the materials to be used in the building, their quality and method of installation, and all details related to the construction of the building.

The architect's job is very complex. He or she is expected to know construction methods, engineering principles and practices, and materials. Architects also must be up to date on new design and construction techniques and procedures. Although architects once spent most of their time designing buildings for the wealthy, they are now more often involved in the design of housing developments,

An architecture student constructs a building model. *(Jeff Greenberg/The Image Works)*

individual dwellings, supermarkets, industrial plants, office build-ings, shopping centers, airport terminals, schools, banks, museums, churches and structures of other religious faiths, and dozens of other types of buildings.

Architects may specialize in any one of a number of fields, includ-ing building appraisal, city planning, teaching, architectural jour-nalism, furniture design, lighting design, or government service. Regardless of the area of specialization, the architect's major task is that of understanding the client's needs and then reconciling them into a meaningful whole.

REQUIREMENTS

High School

To prepare for this career while in high school, take a college pre-paratory program that includes courses in English, mathematics, physics, art (especially freehand drawing), social studies, history, and foreign languages. Courses in business and computer science also will be useful.

Postsecondary Training

Because most state architecture registration boards require a profes-sional degree, high school students are advised, early in their senior year, to apply for admission to a professional program that is accredited by the National Architectural Accrediting Board. Competition to enter these programs is high. Grades, class rank, and aptitude and achieve-ment scores count heavily in determining who will be accepted.

Most schools of architecture offer degrees through either a five-year bachelor's program or a three- or four-year master's program. The majority of architecture students seek out the bachelor's degree in architecture, going from high school directly into a five-year pro-gram. Though this is the fastest route, you should be certain that you want to study architecture. Because the programs are so spe-cialized, it is difficult to transfer to another field of study if you change your mind. The master's degree option allows for more flex-ibility but takes longer to complete. In this case, students first earn a liberal arts degree then continue their training by completing a master's program in architecture. Visit http://www.acsa-arch.org/guide_search/home.aspx for a database of architecture schools in the United States and Canada.

A typical college architecture program includes courses in archi-tectural history and theory, the technical and legal aspects of build-ing design, science, and liberal arts.

Certification or Licensing

All states and the District of Columbia require that individuals be licensed before contracting to provide architectural services in that particular state. Though many work in the field without licensure, only licensed architects are required to take legal responsibility for all work. Using a licensed architect for a project is, therefore, less risky than using an unlicensed one. Architects who are licensed usually take on projects with larger responsibilities and have greater chances to advance to managerial or executive positions.

The requirements for registration include graduation from an accredited school of architecture and three years of practical experience (called an internship) with a licensed architect. After these requirements are met, individuals can take the rigorous Architect Registration Examination. Some states require architects to maintain their licensing through continued education. These individuals may complete a certain number of credits every year or two through seminars, workshops, university classes, self-study courses, or other sources.

In addition to becoming licensed, a growing number of architects choose to obtain certification by the National Council of Architectural Registration Boards. If an architect plans to work in more than one state, obtaining this certification can make it easier to become licensed in different states.

Other Requirements

Architects should be intelligent, observant, responsible, and self-disciplined. They should have a concern for detail and accuracy, be able to communicate effectively both orally and in writing, and be able to accept criticism constructively. Although great artistic ability is not necessary, architects should be able to visualize spatial relationships and have the capacity to solve technical problems. Mathematical ability is also important. In addition, architects should possess organizational skills and leadership qualities and be able to work well with others.

EXPLORING

Most architects will welcome the opportunity to talk with young people interested in entering architecture. You may be able to visit their offices to gain a firsthand knowledge of the type of work they do. You can also visit a design studio of a school of architecture or work for an architect or building contractor during summer vacations. Also, many architecture schools offer summer programs for high school students. Books and magazines on architecture also can give you a broad understanding of the nature of the work and the values of the profession.

EMPLOYERS

Of the 141,200 architects working in the United States, most are employed by architectural or engineering firms or other firms related to the construction industry. About one in five architects, however, are self-employed—the ultimate dream of many people in the profession. A few develop graphic design, interior design, or product specialties. Still others put their training to work in the theater, film, or television fields, or in museums, display firms, and architectural product and materials manufacturing companies. A small number are employed in government agencies such as the Departments of Defense, Interior, and Housing and Urban Development and the General Services Administration.

STARTING OUT

Students entering architecture following graduation start as interns in an architectural firm. As interns, they assist in preparing architectural construction documents. They also handle related details, such as administering contracts, coordinating the work of other professionals on the project, researching building codes and construction materials, and writing specifications. As an alternative to working for an architectural firm, some architecture graduates go into allied fields such as construction, engineering, interior design, landscape architecture, or real estate development.

ADVANCEMENT

Interns and architects alike are given progressively more complex jobs. Architects may advance to supervisory or managerial positions. Some architects become partners in established firms, while others take steps to establish their own practice.

EARNINGS

Architects earned a median annual salary of $70,320 in 2008, according to the U.S. Department of Labor. The lowest paid 10 percent earned less than $41,320 annually, while the highest paid 10 percent earned $119,220 or more.

Well-established architects who are partners in an architectural firm or who have their own businesses generally earn much more than salaried employees. Most employers offer such fringe benefits as health insurance, sick and vacation pay, and retirement plans.

WORK ENVIRONMENT

Architects normally work a 40-hour week. There may be a number of times when they will have to work overtime, especially when under pressure to complete an assignment. Self-employed architects work less regular hours and often meet with clients in their homes or offices during the evening. Architects usually work in comfortable offices, but they may spend a considerable amount of time outside the office visiting clients or viewing the progress of a particular job in the field. Their routines usually vary considerably.

OUTLOOK

Employment in the field is expected to grow faster than the average for all occupations through 2018, according to the U.S. Department of Labor. The number of architects needed will depend on the volume of construction. The construction industry is extremely sensitive to fluctuations in the overall economy, and a bad economic climate could result in layoffs. In the next decade, employment is expected to be best in nonresidential construction. On the positive side, employment of architects is not likely to be affected by the growing use of computer technologies. Rather than replacing architects, computers are being used to enhance the architect's work.

Demographic trends will also play a strong role in fueling employment growth for architects. As a larger percentage of Americans reach the age of 65 and older, architects will be needed to design new health care facilities, nursing homes, and retirement communities. Aging educational facilities will also require the construction of new, larger, and more energy efficient structures. Architects with knowledge of sustainable design techniques should have excellent employment opportunities.

Competition for employment will continue to be strong, particularly in prestigious architectural firms. Openings will not be newly created positions but will become available as the workload increases and established architects transfer to other occupations or leave the field.

FOR MORE INFORMATION

For information on education, jobs, scholarships, and student membership opportunities, contact
American Institute of Architects
1735 New York Avenue, NW
Washington, DC 20006-5292
Tel: 800-242-3837
Email: infocentral@aia.org
http://www.aia.org

For information on education, summer programs for high school students, and student membership opportunities, contact
American Institute of Architecture Students
1735 New York Avenue, NW
Washington, DC 20006-5292
Tel: 202-626-7472
Email: mailbox@aias.org
http://www.aias.org

For information on careers in architecture, visit
ARCHcareers.org
http://www.archcareers.org

For information on schools of architecture, contact
Association of Collegiate Schools of Architecture
1735 New York Avenue, NW
Washington, DC 20006-5292
Tel: 202-783-6500
http://www.acsa-arch.org

For information on certification, contact
National Council of Architectural Registration Boards
1801 K Street, NW, Suite 700-K
Washington, DC 20006-1301
Tel: 202-879-0520
http://www.ncarb.org

INTERVIEW

Ramsay Gourd is the owner of Ramsay Gourd Architects, an architectural firm in Manchester, Vermont. He discussed his career with the editors of Careers in Focus: Construction.

Q. How long have you been an architect?

A. I have been practicing architecture since 1988, when I graduated from Cornell University College of Architecture, Art & Planning. In 1994 I moved to Vermont, where I now have a small practice.

Q. Why did you decide to become an architect?

A. I come from a family of designers. I have always been a strong artist and enjoy problem solving. My interest in working with people on a personal level has helped shape my career and form my practice.

Q. What are the three most important professional qualities for architects?

A. Inherent traits for a good architect are natural artistic talent, creative problem-solving skills, and strength as a visual mathematician.

Q. What do you like most and least about your job?

A. I enjoy most the craft in developing a design and communicating my ideas visually. I like least the way in which computers are being integrated in the field. While they are incredibly powerful tools, we are seeing less and less of the nuance of the ambiguous lines that evolve into thoroughly conceived ideas. It has become too easy to make a drawing that looks good and means little. No matter how much information we put on a drawing, if it is based on a weak concept, it's worth little.

Q. What advice would you give to high school students who are interested in this career?

A. Spend time developing your visual talents. Draw, draw, draw. Learn how to communicate three-dimensional ideas to paper. Learn how to think and see spatially. This is where the difference lies between graphic design and built forms.

Bricklayers and Stonemasons

QUICK FACTS

School Subjects
Mathematics
Technical/shop

Personal Skills
Mechanical/manipulative
Technical/scientific

Work Environment
Primarily outdoors
Primarily multiple locations

Minimum Education Level
High school diploma
Apprenticeship

Salary Range
$24,200 to $41,715 to
$74,110

Certification or Licensing
None available

Outlook
About as fast as the average

DOT
861

GOE
06.02.01

NOC
7281

O*NET-SOC
47-2021.00, 47-2022.00

OVERVIEW

Bricklayers are skilled workers who construct and repair walls, partitions, floors, arches, fireplaces, chimneys, and other structures from brick, concrete block, gypsum block, and precast panels made of terra cotta, structural tile, and other masonry materials. *Stonemasons* build stone walls, floors, piers, and other structures, and they set the decorative stone exteriors of structures such as churches, hotels, and public buildings. Approximately 160,200 bricklayers and stonemasons work in the United States.

HISTORY

Sun-baked clay bricks were used in constructing buildings more than 6,000 years ago in Mesopotamia. In ancient Egypt stone and brick were used in many structures. The Romans introduced masonry construction to the rest of Europe and made innovations in bricklaying, including the use of mortar and different types of bonds, or patterns. As the Roman Empire declined, so did the art of bricklaying. During the period of cathedral building in Europe, from about the 10th century to the 17th century, stonemasons formed guilds in various cities and towns. These guilds functioned much as today's unions do. They had the same categories of workers: apprentices, journeymen, and masters. Not until the great fire of London in 1666 did the English start to use brick again in building. The Chinese also were experts in bricklaying and stonemasonry, the best example of their work being the Great Wall

16

of China. High in the Andes of South America, Incan stoneworkers had perfected their art by the 12th century.

Although some brick houses made of imported bricks were built in Florida by the Spaniards, the first bricks made by Europeans in North America were manufactured in Virginia in 1612. These bricks were handmade from clay, just as they were in ancient times. Machines were not used in the manufacturing of bricks until the mid-18th century. Changes in the content of bricks came shortly afterward. Concrete and cinder blocks were developed at this time, as was structural clay tile.

Today, attractive kinds of brick, called face brick, can be used in places where appearance is especially important. The use of face brick has helped to popularize brick in modern construction. Various colors of brick can be made by using iron oxides, iron sulfides, and other materials. By varying the bond and hue of brick, many interesting artistic effects can be achieved.

Stone is a durable, adaptable material for building purposes, although one of its drawbacks is that it may be much more difficult to cut and transport than alternative materials. Today it remains popular, particularly as a material for enhancing the appearance of important structures like hotels, public buildings, and churches. In modern construction, a covering of stone veneer about two inches thick is applied in various patterns to exterior surfaces of buildings; the veneer is anchored and supported on a steel frame.

THE JOB

When bricklayers and stonemasons begin work on a job, they usually first examine a blueprint or drawing to determine the designer's specifications. Then they measure the work area to fix reference points and guidelines in accordance with the blueprint.

If they are building a wall, bricklayers traditionally start with the corners, or leads, which must be precisely established if the finished structure is to be sound and straight. The corners may be established by more experienced bricklayers, with the task of filling in between the corners left to less experienced workers. Corner posts, or masonry guides, may be used to define the line of the wall, speeding the building process. A first, dry course may be put down without mortar so that the alignment and positioning of the brick can be checked.

Bricklayers use a metal trowel to spread a bed or layer of soft mortar on a prepared base. Then they set the brick into the mortar, tapping and working each brick into the correct position. Excess mortar is cut off, and the mortar joints are smoothed with special tools that give a neat, uniform look to the wall. In walls, each layer, or course, is set so that vertical joints do not line up one on top of another but instead form a pleasing, regular pattern. The work must be continually checked for horizontal and vertical straightness with mason's levels, gauge strips, plumb lines, and other equipment. Sometimes it is necessary to cut and fit brick to size using a power saw or hammer and chisel. Around doors and windows, bricklayers generally use extra steel supports in the wall.

Bricklayers must know how to mix mortar, which is made of cement, sand, and water, and how to spread it so that the joints throughout the structure will be evenly spaced, with a neat appearance. They may have helpers who mix the mortar as well as move materials and scaffolding around the work site as needed.

Some bricklayers specialize in working with one type of masonry material only, such as gypsum block, concrete block, hollow tile used in partitions, or terra-cotta products. Other bricklayers, called *refractory masons,* work in the steel and glass manufacturing industries and specialize in installing firebrick and refractory tile linings of furnaces, kilns, boilers, cupolas, and other high-temperature equipment. Still others are employed to construct manholes and catch basins in sewers.

Stonemasons work with two types of stone: natural cut stone, such as marble, granite, limestone, or sandstone; and artificial stone, which is made to order from concrete, marble chips, or other masonry materials. They set the stone in many kinds of structures, including piers, walls, walks, arches, floors, and curbstones. On some projects, the drawings that stonemasons work from specify where to set certain stones that have been previously identified by number. In such cases, helpers may locate the stones and bring them to the masons. Large stones may have to be hoisted into place with derricks.

In building stone walls, masons begin by setting a first course of stones in a bed of mortar and then build upward by alternating layers of mortar and stone courses. At every stage, they may use leveling devices and plumb lines, correcting the alignment of each stone. They often insert wedges and tap the stones into place with rubber mallets. Once a stone is in good position, masons remove the wedges, fill the gaps with mortar, and smooth the area using a metal tool called a tuck pointer. Large stones may need to be anchored in place with metal brackets that are welded or bolted to the wall.

Similarly, when masons construct stone floors, they begin by spreading mortar. They place stones, adjusting the stones' positions using mallets and crowbars and periodically checking the levelness of the surface. They may cut some stones into smaller pieces to fit, using hammer and chisel or a power saw with a diamond blade.

After all the stones are placed, the masons fill the joints between the stones with mortar and wash off the surface.

Some stonemasons specialize in setting marble. Others work exclusively on setting alberene, which is an acid-resistant soapstone used in industrial settings on floors and for lining vats and tanks. Other specialized stone workers include composition stone applicators, monument setters, patchers, and chimney repairers. *Stone repairers* mend broken slabs made of marble and similar stone.

Bricklayers and stonemasons sometimes use power tools, such as saws and drills, but for the most part they use hand tools, including trowels, jointers, hammers, rulers, chisels, squares, gauge lines, mallets, brushes, and mason's levels.

REQUIREMENTS

High School

As with many jobs, employers of bricklayers and stonemasons will often prefer applicants that have a high school education or at least a GED. Take as many courses as possible in shop, basic mathematics, blueprint reading, and mechanical drawing. Take college prep courses in engineering if your school offers them. It may also help you on the job if you have taken core courses like English and general science and have a driver's license.

A stonemason fits a stone on a church tower. (*James Marshall/The Image Works*)

Another piece of good advice is to join or help form a student chapter of an organization like the National Association of Home Builders. You will get benefits like issues of various journals in the building industry, low-cost admission to the International Builders' Show, and opportunities to take part in exciting activities like visiting construction sites, sponsoring restoration projects at your school, and helping repair homes for the elderly and underprivileged. Visit http://www.hbi.org for more information.

Postsecondary Training

The best way for you to become a bricklayer or stonemason is to complete an apprenticeship. Vocational schools also provide training in these fields. However, many people learn their skills informally on the job simply by observing and helping experienced workers. The disadvantage of this approach is that informal training is likely to be less thorough, and it may take workers much longer to learn the full range of skills necessary for the trade.

Apprenticeship programs are sponsored by contractors or jointly by contractors and unions. Nonunion-sponsored programs are also available. Applicants for apprenticeships need to be at least 17 years old and in good physical condition. As an apprentice, you will spend about three years learning as you work under the supervision of experienced bricklayers or stonemasons. In addition, you will get at least 144 hours of classroom instruction in related subjects, such as blueprint reading, applied mathematics, and layout work. In the work portion of your apprenticeship, you will begin with simple jobs, like carrying materials and building scaffolds. After becoming familiar with initial tasks, you will eventually take part in a broad range of activities. In the course of an apprenticeship, you can become qualified to work with more than one kind of masonry material.

Other Requirements

In bricklaying and stone masonry, you often have to carry materials and sometimes relatively heavy equipment, such as scaffold parts and rows of brick. Since you'll be mixing mortar and laying brick and stone, you must not mind getting dirty and being on your hands and knees.

You should enjoy doing demanding work and be disciplined and motivated enough to do your job without close and constant supervision. Sometimes, you might be presented with building challenges that require either mental or physical aptitude. The ability to get along with coworkers is also important, as many bricklayers and masons work in teams.

EXPLORING

Opportunities are sometimes limited for high school students to directly experience work in the field of bricklaying and stonemasonry. It is fortunate, however, that student groups exist that provide opportunities for experience and exploration. One such group is the National Association of Home Builders Student Chapters Program, which has chapters in high schools and vocational and technical schools. By becoming a member, you get to experience construction firsthand, including bricklaying and stone masonry. Some groups visit construction sites; others participate in repairing homes; others help organize repairs on their own school buildings.

Hands-on experience is one of the best ways to explore the building trades. If you are too young to get such experience, at least contact others who have already started their careers. For example, try to contact participants from the International Masonry Institute's Masonry Camp or visit its Web site (http://www.imiweb.org/educa tion/masonry_camp) to read a blog and comments from participants and view photographs.

EMPLOYERS

Bricklayers and stonemasons are employed in the building industry for such companies as general contractors or specific building contractors, both large and small. Jobs are available across the country but are concentrated in city areas. Those who are skilled in business matters can start their own companies or be contractors; about 24 percent of the approximately 160,200 bricklayers and stonemasons in the United States are self-employed.

STARTING OUT

The two main ways that people start out in these fields are through formal apprenticeship programs and as helpers or laborers who gradually learn their skills on the job. Helper jobs can be found through newspaper want ads and from the local unemployment office. If you want to apply for an apprenticeship, you can get more information from local contractors, the state employment service, and the local office of the International Union of Bricklayers and Allied Craftworkers. The Home Builders Institute can also be of help.

Another option may be to enter a bricklaying program at a vocational school. Such a program combines classroom instruction with work experience. If you've taken classes at a vocational school, its career services office may be able to help you find a job.

ADVANCEMENT

Bricklayers and stonemasons with enough skill and experience may advance to supervisory positions. Some union contracts require a supervisor if three or more workers are employed on a job.

Supervisors sometimes become superintendents at large construction sites. With additional technical training, bricklayers and stonemasons may become cost estimators. *Cost estimators* look at building plans, obtain quotations on masonry material, and prepare and submit bids on the costs of doing the proposed job. Another possible advancement is to become a city or county inspector who checks to see if the work done by contractors meets local building code regulations. Some bricklayers and stonemasons go into business for themselves as contractors.

EARNINGS

According to the U.S. Department of Labor, the median hourly wage of bricklayers was $21.94 in 2008. A person working full time at this pay rate would have annual earnings of approximately $45,630. Earnings for bricklayers ranged from a low of less than $13.26 per hour (approximately $27,590 annually) to a high of more than $35.63 per hour (about $74,110 yearly).

The U.S. Department of Labor reports that the median hourly wage for stonemasons was $18.17 in 2008. This wage translates into annual earnings of approximately $37,800 for full-time work. The lowest paid 10 percent of stonemasons earned less than $11.63 per hour (approximately $24,200 yearly), and the highest paid 10 percent made more than $31.87 hourly (about $66,300 annually).

Of course, earnings for those who work outside can be affected by bad weather, and earnings are lower for workers in areas where the local economy is in a slump. The pay also varies according to geographic region.

The beginning hourly rate for apprentices is about half the rate for experienced workers. In addition to regular pay, various fringe benefits, such as health and life insurance, pensions, and paid vacations, are available to many workers in this field.

WORK ENVIRONMENT

Most bricklayers and stonemasons work 40 hours a week. They are usually paid time and a half for overtime and double time for work on Saturdays, Sundays, and holidays.

Most of the work is done outdoors, where conditions may be dusty, hot, cold, or damp. Often workers must stand on scaffolds that are high off the ground. They may need to bend or stoop constantly to pick up materials. They may be on their feet most of the working day, or they may kneel for long periods.

Some of the hazards in this work include falling off a scaffold, being hit by falling material, and getting injuries common to lifting and handling heavy material. Whereas poor weather conditions used to affect work schedules and job site conditions, protective sheeting is now used to enclose work areas. This sheeting makes it possible to work through most inclement weather.

Apprentices and experienced workers must furnish their own hand tools and measuring devices. Contractors supply the materials for making mortar, scaffolding, lifts, ladders, and other large equipment used in the construction process.

Well-qualified bricklayers and stonemasons can often find work at wages higher than those of most other construction workers, but because the work is seasonal bricklayers and stonemasons must plan carefully to make it through any periods of unemployment.

OUTLOOK

Employment for bricklayers and stonemasons is predicted to grow about as fast as the average for all careers through 2018, according to the U.S. Department of Labor. Job opportunities, however, should be very good since many workers leave the field each year for less strenuous work, retirement, or other reasons. In addition, population and business growth will create the need for new facilities (such as homes, hospitals, long-term care facilities, and offices) and result in a demand for these skilled workers.

During economic downturns, bricklayers and stonemasons, like other workers in construction-related jobs, can expect to have fewer job opportunities and perhaps be laid off.

FOR MORE INFORMATION

This labor union promotes quality construction and builds markets for general contractors. For more information on apprenticeships and training through its National Center for Construction Education and Research, contact
Associated General Contractors of America
2300 Wilson Boulevard, Suite 400
Arlington, VA 22201-5426
Tel: 703-548-3118

Email: info@agc.org
http://www.agc.org

For information on state apprenticeship programs, visit
Employment & Training Administration
U.S. Department of Labor
http://www.doleta.gov

The HBI is the educational arm of the National Association of Home Builders. For more information on education and training programs, contact
Home Builders Institute (HBI)
1201 15th Street NW, 6th Floor
Washington, DC 20005-2842
Tel: 800-795-7955
Email: postmaster@hbi.org
http://www.hbi.org

For information on design and technical assistance as well as information on an annual masonry camp for chosen apprentices, contact
International Masonry Institute
The James Brice House
42 East Street
Annapolis, MD 21401-1731
Tel: 410-280-1305
http://imiweb.org

For information on union membership, contact
International Union of Bricklayers and Allied Craftworkers
620 F Street, NW
Washington, DC 20004-1618
Tel: 888-880-8222
Email: askbac@bacweb.org
http://www.bacweb.org

For information on specialized education and research programs and apprenticeship opportunities, contact
Mason Contractors Association of America
33 South Roselle Road
Schaumburg, IL 60193-1646
Tel: 800-536-2225
http://www.masoncontractors.org

For information on masonry, contact
The Masonry Society
3970 Broadway, Suite 201-D
Boulder, CO 80304-1135
Email: info@masonrysociety.org
http://www.masonrysociety.org

Carpenters

QUICK FACTS

School Subjects
Mathematics
Technical/shop

Personal Skills
Following instructions
Mechanical/manipulative

Work Environment
Indoors and outdoors
Primarily multiple locations

Minimum Education Level
Apprenticeship

Salary Range
$24,240 to $38,940 to
$69,340+

Certification or Licensing
Voluntary

Outlook
About as fast as the average

DOT
860

GOE
06.02.02

NOC
7271

O*NET-SOC
47-2031.00

OVERVIEW

Carpenters cut, shape, level, and fasten together pieces of wood and other construction materials, such as wallboard, plywood, and insulation. Many carpenters construct, remodel, or repair houses and other kinds of buildings. Other carpenters work at construction sites where roads, bridges, docks, boats, mining tunnels, and wooden vats are built. *Rough carpenters* specialize in building the rough framing of a structure, and *finish carpenters* specialize in the finishing details of a structure, such as the trim around doors and windows. Approximately 1.3 million carpenters work in the United States.

HISTORY

Wood has been used as a building material since the dawn of civilization. Tools that resembled modern hand tools first began to be made around 1500 B.C. By the Middle Ages, many of the basic techniques and the essential tools of carpentry were perfected, largely by monks in the early monasteries.

Over time, many specialties developed in the field of carpentry. The primary work came from building construction. Buildings were mostly built with braced-frame construction, which made use of large, heavy timbers held together with mortised joints and diagonal bracing. In this kind of construction, carpenters were often the principal workers on a house or other building.

Carpenters also were responsible for many of the necessities that kept their towns running from day to day. Pit sawyers milled lumber from trees. Carts and wagons called for wheelwrights, who fabricated wheels and axles, and then, as transportation became more sophisticated, coach- and wagonmakers appeared. The increased use of brass and iron led to work for patternmakers, who created the wooden forms that were the first step in casting. On the domestic front, cabinetmakers and joiners were skilled in building furniture or creating interior trimwork.

It is no surprise that the role of carpenters has continued to change, largely due to the rise of machine technology. Since the mid-19th century, balloon-frame construction, which makes use of smaller and lighter pieces of wood, has simplified the construction process, and concrete and steel have replaced wood for many purposes, especially in floors and roofs. Power tools have replaced hand tools in many instances. But as some carpentry tasks in building construction have become easier, other new jobs, such as making forms for poured concrete, have added to the importance of carpenters at construction sites. Carpentry continues to be an important and necessary trade.

THE JOB

Carpenters remain the largest group of workers in the building trades—there are approximately 1.3 million carpenters in the United States today. Most work for contractors involved in building, repairing, and remodeling buildings and other structures. Manufacturing firms, schools, stores, and government bodies employ most other carpenters.

Carpenters do two basic kinds of work: rough carpentry and finish carpentry. *Rough carpenters* construct and install temporary structures and supports and wooden structures used in industrial settings, as well as parts of buildings that are usually covered up when the rooms are finished. Among the structures built by such carpenters are scaffolds for other workers to stand on, chutes used as channels for wet concrete, forms for concrete foundations, and timber structures that support machinery. In buildings, they may put up the frame and install rafters, joists, subflooring, wall sheathing, prefabricated wall panels and windows, and many other components.

Finish carpenters install hardwood flooring, staircases, shelves, cabinets, trim on windows and doors, and other woodwork and hardware that make the building look complete, inside and outside. Finish carpentry requires especially careful, precise workmanship, since the result must have a good appearance in addition to being sturdy. Many carpenters who are employed by building contractors do both rough and finish work on buildings.

Although they do many different tasks in different settings, carpenters generally follow the same basic steps. First, they review blueprints or plans (or they obtain instructions from a supervisor) to determine the dimensions of the structure to be built and the types of materials to be used. Sometimes local building codes mandate how a structure should be built, so carpenters need to know about such regulations.

Using rulers, framing squares, chalk lines, and other measuring and marking equipment, carpenters lay out how the work will be done. Using hand and power tools, they cut and shape the wood, plywood, fiberglass, plastic, or other materials. Then they nail, screw, glue, or staple the pieces together. Finally, they use levels, plumb bobs, rulers, and squares to check their work, and they make any necessary adjustments. Sometimes carpenters work with prefabricated units for components such as wall panels or stairs. Installing these can be one of a carpenter's less complicated tasks, because much less layout, cutting, and assembly work is needed.

Carpenters who work outside of the building construction field may do a variety of installation and maintenance jobs, such as repairing furniture and installing ceiling tiles or exterior siding on buildings. Other carpenters specialize in building, repairing, or modifying ships, wooden boats, wooden railroad trestles, timber framing in mine shafts, woodwork inside railcars, storage tanks and vats, or stage sets in theaters.

Carpenters need manual dexterity, good hand-eye coordination, and a strong sense of balance. *(James Marshall/The Image Works)*

REQUIREMENTS

High School

A high school education is not mandatory to be a carpenter, but most contractors and developers prefer applicants with a diploma or a GED. A good high school background for prospective carpenters would include carpentry and woodworking courses as well as other shop classes, applied mathematics, mechanical drawing, and blueprint reading.

Postsecondary Training

As an aspiring carpenter, you can acquire the skills of your trade in various ways, through formal training programs and through informal on-the-job training. Of the different ways to learn, an apprenticeship is considered the best, as it provides a more thorough and complete foundation for a career as a carpenter than do other kinds of training. However, the limited number of available apprenticeships means that not all carpenters can learn the trade this way.

You can pick up skills informally on the job while you work as a carpenter's helper—and many carpenters enter the field this way. You will begin with little or no training and gradually learn as you work under the supervision of experienced carpenters. The skills that you will develop as a helper will depend on the jobs that your employers contract to do. Working for a small contracting company, a beginner may learn about relatively few kinds of carpentry tasks. On the other hand, a large contracting company may offer a wider variety of learning opportunities. Becoming a skilled carpenter by this method can take much longer than an apprenticeship, and the completeness of the training varies. While some individuals are waiting for an apprenticeship to become available they may work as helpers to gain experience in the field.

Some people first learn about carpentry while serving in the military. Others learn skills in vocational educational programs offered in trade schools and through correspondence courses. Vocational programs can be very good, especially as a supplement to other practical training. But without additional hands-on instruction, vocational school graduates may not be adequately prepared to get many jobs in the field because some programs do not provide sufficient opportunity for students to practice and perfect their carpentry skills.

Apprenticeships, which will provide you with the most comprehensive training available, usually last four years. They are administered by employer groups and by local chapters of labor unions that organize carpenters. Applicants must meet the specific requirements of local apprenticeship committees. Typically, you must be at least

17 years old, have a high school diploma, and be able to show that you have some aptitude for carpentry.

Apprenticeships combine on-the-job work experience with classroom instruction in a planned, systematic program. Initially, you will work at such simple tasks as building concrete forms, doing rough framing, and nailing subflooring. Toward the end of your training, you may work on finishing trimwork, fitting hardware, hanging doors, and building stairs. In the course of this experience, you will become familiar with the tools, materials, techniques, and equipment of the trade, and you will learn how to do layout, framing, finishing, and other basic carpentry jobs.

The work experience segment of an apprenticeship is supplemented by about 144 hours of classroom instruction per year. Some of this instruction concerns the correct use and maintenance of tools, safety practices, first aid, building code requirements, and the properties of different construction materials. Other subjects you will study include the principles of layout, blueprint reading, shop mathematics, and sketching. Both on the job and in the classroom, you will learn how to work effectively with members of other skilled building trades.

Certification or Licensing

The United Brotherhood of Carpenters and Joiners of America (UBCJA), the national union for the industry, offers certification courses in a variety of specialty skills. These courses teach the ins and outs of advanced skills—like scaffold construction—that help to ensure worker safety, while at the same time giving workers ways to enhance their abilities and so qualify for better jobs. Some job sites require all workers to undergo training in safety techniques and guidelines specified by the Occupational Safety and Health Administration. Workers who have not passed these courses are considered ineligible for jobs at these sites.

Other Requirements

In general, as a carpenter, you will need to have manual dexterity, good hand-eye coordination, and a good sense of balance. You will need to be in good physical condition, as the work involves a great deal of physical activity. Stamina is much more important than physical strength. On the job, you may have to climb, stoop, kneel, crouch, and reach as well as deal with the challenges of weather.

EXPLORING

Beyond classes such as woodshop or mechanical drawing, there are a number of real-world ways to begin exploring a career in carpentry and the construction trades. Contact trade organizations like the National Association of Home Builders or the Associated General Contractors of America; both sponsor student chapters around the country. Consider volunteering for an organization like Habitat for Humanity; Its Youth Programs accept volunteers between the ages of five and 25, and their group building projects provide hands-on experience. If your school has a drama department, look into it—building sets can be a fun way to learn simple carpentry skills. In addition, your local home improvement store is likely to sponsor classes that teach a variety of skills useful around the house; some of these will focus on carpentry.

A less direct method to find out about carpentry is via television and the Internet. PBS and some cable stations show how-to programs—such as *This Old House* and *The New Yankee Workshop*—that feature the work of carpenters. Both shows also offer companion Web sites that can be found at http://www.thisoldhouse.com/toh and http://www.newyankee.com, respectively.

EMPLOYERS

Carpenters account for a large group of workers in the building trades, holding approximately 1.3 million jobs. About 32 percent of carpenters work for general-building contractors, and 22 percent work for specialty contractors. About 32 percent are self-employed.

Some carpenters work for manufacturing firms, government agencies, retail and wholesale establishments, or schools. Others work in the shipbuilding, aircraft, or railroad industries. Still others work in the arts, for theaters and movie and television production companies as set builders, or for museums or art galleries, building exhibits.

STARTING OUT

Information about available apprenticeships can be obtained by contacting the local office of the state employment service, area contractors that hire carpenters, or the local offices of the United Brotherhood of Carpenters, which cooperates in sponsoring apprenticeship programs. Helper jobs that can be filled by beginners without special training in carpentry may be advertised in newspaper classified ads or with the state employment service. You also might consider contacting potential employers directly.

ADVANCEMENT

Once an applicant has completed and met all the requirements of apprenticeship training, he or she will be considered a jour-

Habitat for Humanity

Habitat for Humanity "seeks to eliminate poverty housing and homelessness from the world and to make decent shelter a matter of conscience and action." If you are interested in carpentry or another trade, volunteering with this organization is an excellent way to get experience and help people who are less fortunate than you. Opportunities are available throughout the United States and the world. Here are just a few of Habitat for Humanity's accomplishments since it was founded in 1976:

- Has built more than 300,000 houses
- Has provided more than 1.5 million people in more than 3,000 communities with housing
- Operates in more than 90 countries

For more information, contact Habitat for Humanity International, 121 Habitat Street Americus, GA 31709-3498, Tel: 800-HABITAT, ext. 2412, Email: youthprograms@habitat.org, http://www.habitat.org.

neyman carpenter. With sufficient experience, journeymen may be promoted to positions responsible for supervising the work of other carpenters. If a carpenter's background includes exposure to a broad range of construction activities, he or she may eventually advance to a position as a general construction supervisor. A carpenter who is skillful at mathematical computations and has a good knowledge of the construction business may become an *estimator.* An experienced carpenter might one day go into business for himself or herself, doing repair or construction work as an independent contractor.

EARNINGS

According to the U.S. Department of Labor, carpenters had median hourly earnings of $18.72 in 2008. Someone making this wage and working full time for the year would have an income of approximately $38,940. The lowest paid 10 percent of carpenters earned less than $11.66 per hour (or approximately $24,240 per year), and the highest paid 10 percent made more than $33.34 hourly (approximately $69,340 annually). It is important to note, however, that these annual salaries are for full-time work. Many carpenters, like others in the building trades, have periods of unemployment during the year, and their incomes may not match these.

Starting pay for apprentices is about 50 percent of a journeyman carpenter's earnings. The wage is increased periodically so that by the fourth year of training apprentice pay is 90 to 95 percent of the journeyman carpenter's rate.

Fringe benefits, such as health insurance, pension funds, and paid vacations, are available to most workers in this field and vary with local union contracts. In general, benefits are more likely to be offered on jobs staffed by union workers.

WORK ENVIRONMENT

Carpenters may work either indoors or outdoors. If they do rough carpentry, they will probably do most of their work outdoors. Carpenters may have to work on high scaffolding, or in a basement making cement forms. A construction site can be noisy, dusty, hot, cold, or muddy. Carpenters can expect to be physically active throughout the day, constantly standing, stooping, climbing, and reaching. Some of the possible hazards of the job include being hit by falling objects, falling off scaffolding or a ladder, straining muscles, and getting cuts and scrapes on fingers and hands. Carpenters who follow recommended safety practices and procedures minimize these hazards.

Work in the construction industry involves changing from one job location to another, and from time to time being laid off because of poor weather, shortages of materials, or simply lack of jobs. Carpenters must be able to arrange their finances so that they can make it through long periods of unemployment.

Though it is not required, many carpenters are members of a union such as the UBCJA. Among many other services, such as the certification courses mentioned previously, the union works with employers, seeking to ensure that members receive equitable pay and work in safe conditions.

OUTLOOK

Although the U.S. Department of Labor predicts that employment for carpenters will increase about as fast as the average for all occupations through 2018, job opportunities for carpenters are expected to be very strong. This is because replacement carpenters are needed for the large number of experienced carpenters who leave the field every year for work that is less strenuous. Replacement workers are also needed for the fair amount of workers just starting out in the field who decide to move on to more comfortable occupations. And, of course, replacements are needed for those who retire. Increased home building and construction of hotels, restaurants, and other businesses, as well as roads and bridges; home modifications for the growing elderly population; two-income couples' desire for larger homes; and the growing population of all ages should contribute to the demand for carpenters.

Factors that will hold down employment growth in the field include the use of more prefabricated building parts and improved tools that make construction easier and faster. In addition, a weak economy has a major impact on the building industry, causing companies and individuals to put off expensive building projects until better times. Carpenters with good all-around skills, such as those who have completed apprenticeships, will have the best job opportunities even in difficult times.

FOR MORE INFORMATION

For information on activities and student chapters, contact
Associated General Contractors of America
2300 Wilson Boulevard, Suite 400
Arlington, VA 22201-5426
Tel: 703-548-3118
Email: info@agc.org
http://www.agc.org

For information on state apprenticeship programs, visit
Employment & Training Administration
U.S. Department of Labor
http://www.doleta.gov

Habitat for Humanity is an internationally recognized nonprofit organization dedicated to the elimination of poverty housing. For information on programs and local chapters found all over the United States, contact
Habitat for Humanity International
121 Habitat Street
Americus, GA 31709-3498
Tel: 800-HABITAT, ext. 2412
Email: youthprograms@habitat.org
http://www.habitat.org

*For information on apprenticeships, training programs, and general
information about trends in the industry, contact*
Home Builders Institute
1201 15th Street, NW, 6th Floor
Washington, DC 20005-2842
Tel: 800-795-7955
Email: postmaster@hbi.org
http://www.hbi.org

*For information about careers in the construction trades and stu-
dent chapters, contact*
National Association of Home Builders
1201 15th Street, NW
Washington, DC 20005-2842
Tel: 800-368-5242
http://www.nahb.com

For information on union membership and apprenticeships, contact
United Brotherhood of Carpenters and Joiners of America
Carpenters Training Fund
6801 Placid Street
Las Vegas, NV 89119-4205
http://www.carpenters.org

Cement Masons

QUICK FACTS

School Subjects
Chemistry
Mathematics
Technical/shop

Personal Skills
Mechanical/manipulative
Technical/scientific

Work Environment
Primarily outdoors
Primarily multiple locations

Minimum Education Level
Apprenticeship

Salary Range
$22,920 to $35,080 to
$63,020+

Certification or Licensing
None available

Outlook
About as fast as the average

DOT
844

GOE
06.02.01

NOC
7282

O*NET-SOC
47-2051.00

OVERVIEW

Cement masons, also known as *concrete masons,* usually work for contractors in the building and construction industries. Cement masons apply the concrete surfaces in many different kinds of construction projects, ranging from small patios and sidewalks to highways, dams, and airport runways. Cement masons' responsibilities include building forms for holding the concrete, determining the correct mixture of ingredients, and making sure the structure is suitable to the environment. Roughly 207,800 cement masons, concrete finishers, segmental pavers, and terrazzo workers are employed in the United States.

HISTORY

Cement has been used for thousands of years as a hard building material. It is made by mixing such elements as powdered alumina, silica, and limestone with water to make a solid mass. One could say that the ancient Egyptians and the Greeks were cement masons—both groups made cements. The most effective masons were perhaps the Romans, for they developed a kind of cement made from slaked lime and volcanic ash and used it throughout Europe in building roads, aqueducts, bridges, and other structures. After the collapse of the Roman Empire, however, the art of making cement practically disappeared.

In the 18th century an English engineer named John Smeaton developed a cement that set even under water. Smeaton successfully used this cement in building the famous Eddystone Lighthouse in Devon, England. Later it was used in some parts of the Erie Canal, the waterway built to connect the Great Lakes and New York City.

Joseph Aspdin, an English stonemason, developed the first port-land cement mixture in 1824 by burning and grinding together lime-stone and clay. He called his product "portland" cement because it resembled the limestone quarried on the Isle of Portland. It soon became the most widely used cement because of its strength and resistance to water. The first American portland cement plant was built in 1871. Cement manufactured today is essentially made of the same material as Aspdin's portland cement.

Masons seldom use cement by itself in large quantities. More often, they mix it with another material, like sand, to form a mortar to be used in structures such as brick walls and buildings. When they mix it with gravel or crushed rock, it forms concrete, a cheap, versatile, durable structural material. Today concrete is one of the most widely used building materials in the world. With the development of ways to reinforce concrete with metal and the appropriate machinery for handling it, concrete has become useful in building many structures, including fence posts, swimming pools, sculptures, roofs, bridges, highways, dams, helicopter pads, and missile launching sites.

THE JOB

The principal work of cement masons, also known as concrete masons, is to put into place and then smooth and finish concrete surfaces in a variety of different construction projects. Sometimes they add colors to the concrete to change its appearance or chemicals to speed up or slow down the amount of time that the concrete takes to harden. They use various tools to create specified surface textures on fresh concrete before it sets. They may also fabricate beams, col-umns, or panels of concrete.

Cement masons must know their materials well. They must be able to judge how long different concrete mixtures will take to set and how factors such as temperature and wind will affect the curing, or hardening, of the cement. They need to be able to recognize these effects by examining and touching the concrete. They need to know about the strengths of different kinds of concrete and how different surface appearances are produced.

Cement masons should understand the materials they work with and be familiar with blueprint reading, applied mathematics, build-ing code regulations, and the procedures involved in estimating the costs and quantities of materials.

On a construction job, the preparation of the site where the con-crete will be poured is important. Cement masons begin by setting up the forms that will hold the wet concrete until it hardens into the desired shape. The forms must be properly aligned and allow for the correct dimensions, as specified in the original design. In some structures, reinforcing steel rods or mesh are set into place after the forms are put in position. The cement masons then pour or direct the pouring of the concrete into the forms so that it flows smoothly. The cement masons or their helpers spread and tamp the fresh concrete into place. Then they level the surface by moving a straightedge back and forth across the top of the forms.

Using a large wooden trowel called a bull float, cement masons begin the smoothing operation. This process covers up the larger particles in the wet concrete and brings to the surface the fine cement paste in the mixture. On projects where curved edges are desired, cement masons may use an edger or radius tool, guiding it around the edge between the form and the concrete. They may make grooves or joints at intervals in the surface to help control cracking.

The process continues with more finishing work, done either by hand with a small metal trowel or with a power trowel. This smoothing gets out most remaining irregularities on the surface. To obtain a nonslip texture on driveways, sidewalks, and similar projects, cement masons may pass a brush or broom across or embed pebbles in the surface. Afterward, the concrete must cure to reach its proper strength—a process that can take up to a week.

On structures such as walls and columns with exposed surfaces, cement masons must leave a smooth and uniform finish after the forms are removed. To achieve this, they may rub down high spots with an abrasive material, chip out rough or defective spots with a chisel and hammer, and fill low areas with cement paste. They may finish off the exposed surface with a coating of a cement mixture to create an even, attractive appearance.

Cement masons use a variety of hand and power tools, ranging from simple chisels, hammers, trowels, edgers, and leveling devices to pneumatic chisels, concrete mixers, and troweling machines. Smaller projects, such as sidewalks and patios, may be done by hand, but on large-scale projects, such as highways, power-operated floats and finishing equipment are necessary. Although power equipment can speed up many tasks, most projects have corners or other inaccessible areas that require hand work.

Various cement specialists have jobs that involve covering, leveling, and smoothing cement and concrete surfaces. Among them are *concrete-stone finishers,* who work with ornamental stone and concrete surfaces; *concrete rubbers,* who polish concrete surfaces; and *nozzle cement sprayers,* who use spray equipment to apply cement mixtures to surfaces.

Poured concrete wall technicians are an occupational group related to cement masons. These workers use surveying instruments to mark construction sites for excavation and to set up and true (that is, align correctly) concrete forms. They direct the pouring of concrete to form walls of buildings, and, after removing the forms, they may water-proof lower walls and lay drainage tile to promote drainage away from the building. Unlike cement masons, however, poured concrete wall technicians generally receive at least two years of technical training in such subjects as surveying and construction methods.

REQUIREMENTS
High School
Cement masons with a high school diploma or GED have an advantage in the job market. Take mathematics courses, and choose shop classes like mechanical drawing and blueprint reading if your school offers these; if it does not offer these specifically, ask your teachers which classes are similar to them. It may also help you on the job if you have taken core courses like English and general science and have a driver's license.

Sometimes, a high school diploma may not be required, but you should have at least taken some kind of vocational-technical classes. If you have no special skills or experience, you might find work as a helper and gradually learn the trade informally over an unspecified number of years by working with experienced masons. In considering applicants for helper jobs, most employers prefer to hire people who are at least 18 and in good physical condition.

Postsecondary Training
It is recommended that you first work as an apprentice to acquire the necessary skills for being a cement mason. Apprenticeships provide balanced, in-depth training. Such full-time programs often last two to three years, and they are usually jointly sponsored by local contractors and unions. If you want to apply for an apprenticeship program, you might need to be approved by the local joint labor-management apprenticeship committee. You also might have to take a written test and pass a physical examination.

Training consists of a combination of planned work experience and classroom instruction. On the job as an apprentice, you will learn about the tools and materials of the trade, layout work and finishing techniques, grinding and paving, and job safety. Further classroom instruction involves around 144 hours each year in such related subjects as mathematics, blueprint reading, architectural drawing, procedures for estimating materials and costs, and local building regulations.

Other Requirements

As a cement mason, you will be involved in a great amount of physical, often strenuous, work. You may be required to show your physical fitness by, for example, lifting a 100-pound sack of sand to your shoulder height and carrying it 50 feet.

You should enjoy demanding work and be disciplined and motivated enough to do your job without close and constant supervision. The ability to get along with coworkers is important, as most cement masons work in teams. Also, as mentioned, you should have a valid driver's license.

EXPLORING

Since this job involves using your hands to build surfaces and forms, you might like working as a cement mason if you enjoy building sculptures or structures. But you also have to use your head—you can learn more about your mental aptitude for this kind of work by taking courses like general mathematics, drafting, and various shop classes. In addition, try to find a summer job on a local construction crew to gain valuable firsthand experience. Some people are introduced to the building construction trades, including the work of cement masons, while they are serving in the military, especially with the U.S. Army Corps of Engineers.

To gain practical experience in this field, ask your local parks department if you can help or at least watch workers making playground areas and skateboard hills. Keep your eyes open for construction and sidewalk work going on in your neighborhood and ask if you can watch from a safe distance.

EMPLOYERS

Approximately 207,800 cement masons, concrete finishers, segmental pavers, and terrazzo workers are employed in the United States. Most cement masons are employed by concrete contractors or general contractors in the building and construction industries to help build roads, shopping malls, factories, and many other structures. Some cement masons work for large contractors for such big operations as utility companies and public works departments; others work for small contractors to construct buildings such as apartment complexes, shopping malls, and schools. Cement masons who are disciplined and skilled enough in the trade and in business may have the goal of one day starting their own companies, perhaps specializing in walkways, swimming pools, or building foundations.

STARTING OUT

You don't have to attend college to become a cement mason. After graduating from high school or getting a GED, you can either go through a formal apprenticeship training program or get work that offers the opportunity for on-the-job training. For information about becoming an apprentice cement mason, contact local cement contractors, the offices of your state's employment service, or the area headquarters of one of the unions that organize cement masons. Many cement masons are members of either the Operative Plasterers' and Cement Masons' International Association or the International Union of Bricklayers and Allied Craftworkers. Search for Web sites in the construction and trades industries. For example, the Oregon Building Congress has a site (http://www.obcweb.com) that gives information on career descriptions and wages and applying for its apprenticeships.

If you want a job as a trainee, get in touch with contractors in your area who may be hiring helpers. Follow up on job leads from the state employment service and newspaper classified ads.

ADVANCEMENT

Once a beginning cement mason has gained some skills and become efficient in the trade, he or she can specialize in a certain phase of the work. A cement mason may become, for example, a lip-curb finisher, an expansion joint finisher, or a concrete paving-finishing machine operator.

An experienced mason with good judgment, planning skills, and the ability to deal with people can try advancing to a supervisory position. Supervisors with a broad understanding of other construction trades may eventually become *job superintendents,* who are in charge of the whole range of activities at the job site. A cement mason may also become an *estimator* for concrete contractors, calculating materials requirements and labor costs. A self-disciplined and highly motivated cement mason can eventually go into business on his or her own by opening a company to do small projects like sidewalks and patios.

EARNINGS

The earnings of cement masons vary widely according to factors such as geographic location, whether they do much overtime work, and how much bad weather or local economic conditions reduce the number of hours worked. Nonunion workers generally receive lower wage rates than union workers. The U.S. Department of Labor reports that in 2008 cement masons earned a median wage of $16.87 per hour. A mason doing steady, full-time work at this wage would earn $35,080 annually. The department also reports that at the low end of the pay scale 10 percent of masons earned less than $11.02 per hour (or less than $22,920 annually). At the high end, 10 percent earned more than $30.30 hourly (more than $63,020 yearly). Since the amount of time spent working is limited by weather conditions, many workers' earnings vary from these figures. Apprentices start at wages that are approximately 50–60 percent of a fully qualified mason's wage. They receive periodic raises, so in the last phase of training, their wage is between 90 and 95 percent of the experienced worker's pay.

Benefits for cement masons typically include overtime pay, health insurance, and a pension plan.

WORK ENVIRONMENT

Cement masons do strenuous work, and they need to have good stamina. Many work outdoors and with other workers. Although cement masons might not work much in rainy and snowy conditions because cement cannot be poured in such weather, they might frequently work overtime, because once the cement has been poured, the finishing operations must be completed quickly. Temporary heated shelters are sometimes used to extend the time when work can be done.

Masons work in a variety of locations—sometimes on the ground, sometimes on ladders and scaffolds. Cement masons may need to lift or push weights, and they often kneel, bend, and stoop. To protect their knees, they routinely wear kneepads; they might also need to wear water-repellent boots and protective clothing.

Common hazards on the job include falling off ladders, being hit by falling objects, having muscle strains, and getting rough hands from contact with wet concrete. By exercising caution and following established job safety practices, masons minimize their exposure to hazardous conditions.

Although most contractors hire workers for 40-hour weeks, many jobs are limited by weather conditions. Masons sometimes have unexpected days off because of rain or snow. Then employers may expect masons to help catch up by working longer than eight hours on days when the weather permits.

OUTLOOK

According to the U.S. Department of Labor, employment for cement masons should grow about as fast as the average for all careers through 2018. Work opportunities for masons should be good, since the number of trained workers is relatively small. In addition, construction activity is expected to expand during this period, and concrete will be an important building material, especially in nonresidential building and construction and in both nonresidential and residential construction projects in hurricane-prone areas. Cement masons will be in demand to help build roads, bridges, buildings, subways, shopping malls, and many other structures. Although the productivity of masons will be improved by the introduction of better tools and materials (resulting in the need for fewer workers), cement masons will be needed to replace those who leave the field for retirement or other occupations.

In areas where the local economy is thriving and there are plenty of building projects, there may be occasional shortages of cement masons. At other times, even skilled masons may experience periods of unemployment because of downturns in the economy and declining levels of construction activity.

FOR MORE INFORMATION

For information on apprenticeship and training programs, contact
Associated General Contractors of America
2300 Wilson Boulevard, Suite 400
Arlington, VA 22201-5426
Tel: 703-548-3118
Email: info@agc.org
http://www.agc.org

For information on state apprenticeship programs, visit
Employment & Training Administration
U.S. Department of Labor
http://www.doleta.gov

For information on its annual masonry camp for chosen apprentices, contact
International Masonry Institute
The James Brice House
42 East Street
Annapolis, MD 21401-1731

Tel: 410-280-1305
http://imiweb.org

For information on union membership, contact
International Union of Bricklayers and Allied Craftworkers
620 F Street, NW
Washington, DC 20004-1618
Tel: 888-880-8222
Email: askbac@bacweb.org
http://www.bacweb.org

For information on education and research programs and apprenticeships, contact
Mason Contractors Association of America
33 South Roselle Road
Schaumburg, IL 60193-1646
Tel: 800-536-2225
http://www.masoncontractors.org

For information on masonry, contact
The Masonry Society
3970 Broadway, Suite 201-D
Boulder, CO 80304-1135
Email: info@masonrysociety.org
http://www.masonrysociety.org

For information on apprenticeship and training programs, contact
**Operative Plasterers' and Cement Masons' International
    Association**
11720 Beltsville Drive, Suite 700
Beltsville, MD 20705-3104
Tel: 301-623-1000
Email: opcmiaintl@opcmia.org
http://www.opcmia.org

Civil Engineers

OVERVIEW

Civil engineers are involved in the design and construction of the physical structures that make up our surroundings, such as roads, bridges, buildings, and harbors. Civil engineering involves theoretical knowledge applied to the practical planning of the layout of cities, towns, and other communities. It is concerned with modifying the natural environment and building new environments to better the lifestyles of the general public. Civil engineers are also known as *structural engineers*. There are approximately 278,400 civil engineers in the United States.

HISTORY

One might trace the evolution of civil engineering methods by considering the building and many reconstructions of England's London Bridge. In Roman and medieval times, several bridges made of timber were built over the Thames River. Around the end of the 12th century, these were rebuilt into 19 narrow arches mounted on piers. A chapel was built on one of the piers, and two towers were built for defense. A fire damaged the bridge around 1212, yet the surrounding area was considered a preferred place to live and work, largely because it was the only bridge over which one could cross the river. The structure was rebuilt many times during later centuries using different materials and designs. By 1830 it had only five arches. More than a century later, the center span of the bridge was remodeled, and part of it was actually transported to the United States to be set up as a tourist attraction.

Working materials for civil engineers have changed during many centuries. For instance, bridges, once made of timber, then of iron and

QUICK FACTS

School Subjects
Mathematics
Physics

Personal Skills
Leadership/management
Technical/scientific

Work Environment
Indoors and outdoors
Primarily multiple locations

Minimum Education Level
Bachelor's degree

Salary Range
$48,140 to $74,600 to
$115,630

Certification or Licensing
Recommended

Outlook
Faster than the average

DOT
055

GOE
02.07.04

NOC
2131

O*NET-SOC
17-2051.00

steel, are today made mainly with concrete that is reinforced with steel. The high strength of the material is necessary because of the abundance of cars and other heavy vehicles that travel over the bridges.

As the population continues to grow and communities become more complex, structures must be remodeled and repaired. New highways, buildings, and airstrips must be designed to accommodate public needs. Today, many civil engineers are involved in the design and construction of water treatment plants, water purification plants, and toxic waste sites. Increasing concern about the natural environment is also evident in the growing number of engineers working on such projects as preservation of wetlands, maintenance of national forests, and restoration of sites around land mines, oil wells, and industrial factories.

THE JOB

Civil engineers use their knowledge of materials science, engineering theory, economics, and demographics to devise, construct, and maintain our physical surroundings. They apply their understanding of other branches of science—such as hydraulics, geology, and physics—to design the optimal blueprint for the project.

Feasibility studies are conducted by *surveying and mapping engineers* to determine the best sites and approaches for construction. They extensively investigate the chosen sites to verify that the ground and other surroundings are amenable to the proposed project. These engineers use sophisticated equipment, such as satellites and other electronic instruments, to measure the area and conduct underground probes for bedrock and groundwater. They determine the optimal places where explosives should be blasted in order to cut through rock.

Many civil engineers work strictly as consultants on projects, advising their clients. These consultants usually specialize in one area of the industry, such as water systems, transportation systems, or housing structures. Clients include individuals, corporations, and the government. Consultants will devise an overall design for the proposed project, perhaps a nuclear power plant commissioned by an electric company. They will estimate the cost of constructing the plant, supervise the feasibility studies and site investigations, and advise the client on whom to hire for the actual labor involved. Consultants are also responsible for such details as accuracy of drawings and quantities of materials to order.

Other civil engineers work mainly as contractors and are responsible for the actual building of the structure; they are known as *construction engineers*. They interpret the consultants' designs and follow through with the best methods for getting the work done, usually working directly at the construction site. Contractors are responsible for scheduling the work, buying the materials, maintaining surveys of the progress of the work, and choosing the machines and other equipment used for construction. During construction, these civil engineers must supervise the labor and make sure the work is completed correctly and efficiently. After the project is finished, they must set up a maintenance schedule and periodically check the structure for a certain length of time. Later, the task of ongoing maintenance and repair is often transferred to local engineers.

Civil engineers may be known by their area of specialization. *Transportation engineers,* for example, are concerned mainly with the construction of highways and mass transit systems, such as subways and commuter rail lines. When devising plans for subways, engineers are responsible for considering the tunneling that is involved. *Pipeline engineers* are specialized civil engineers who are involved with the movement of water, oil, and gas through miles of pipeline.

REQUIREMENTS

High School
Because a bachelor's degree is considered essential in the field, high school students interested in civil engineering must follow a college prep curriculum. Students should focus on mathematics (algebra, trigonometry, geometry, and calculus), the sciences (physics and chemistry), computer science, and English and the humanities (history, economics, and sociology). Students should also aim for honors-level courses.

Postsecondary Training
In addition to completing the core engineering curriculum (including mathematics, science, drafting, and computer applications), students can choose their specialty from the following types of courses: structural analysis, materials design and specification, geology, hydraulics, surveying and design graphics, soil mechanics, and oceanography. Bachelor's degrees can be achieved through a number of programs: a four- or five-year accredited college or university; two years in a community college engineering program plus two or three years in a college or university; or five or six years in a co-op program (attending classes for part of the year and working in an engineering-related job for the rest of the year). About 30 percent of civil engineering students go on to receive a master's degree. Visit http://www.asce.org/community/educational/instlist.cfm for a list of civil engineering programs.

Certification or Licensing
Most civil engineers go on to study and qualify for a professional engineer (PE) license. It is required before one can work on projects

Earnings for Civil Engineers by Industry, 2008

Field	Mean Annual Earnings
Federal government	$85,970
Architectural, engineering, and related services	$79,880
Nonresidential building construction	$78,630
Local government	$76,830
State government	$71,660

Source: U.S. Department of Labor

affecting property, health, or life. Because many engineering jobs are found in government specialties, most engineers take the necessary steps to obtain the license. Requirements are different for each state—they involve educational, practical, and teaching experience. Applicants must take an examination on a specified date.

Other Requirements

Basic personal characteristics often found in civil engineers are avid curiosity; passion for mathematics and science; aptitude for problem solving, both alone and with a team; and an ability to visualize multidimensional, spatial relationships.

EXPLORING

High school students can become involved in civil engineering by attending a summer camp or study program in the field. For example, North Carolina State University has an Engineering Summer Program for high school students who have completed their sophomore or junior years. The program is "designed to introduce students to engineering problem-solving techniques through hands-on laboratory experience, lectures, and field visits." A program for students interested in civil engineering is available. Visit http://www.engr.ncsu.edu/summerprograms for more information.

Additionally, the American Society of Civil Engineers offers a wealth of information about careers at its Web site (http://www.asce.org).

After high school, another way to learn about civil engineering duties is to work on a construction crew that is involved in the actual building of a project designed and supervised by engineers. Such hands-on experience would provide an opportunity to work near many types of civil engineering workers. Try to work on highway crews or even in housing construction.

EMPLOYERS

Nearly half of the 278,400 civil engineers employed in the United States work for companies involved in architectural and engineering consulting services. Others work for government agencies at the local, state, or federal level. A small percentage are self-employed, running their own consulting businesses.

STARTING OUT

To establish a career as a civil engineer, one must first receive a bachelor's degree in engineering or another appropriate scientific field. College career services offices are often the best sources of employment for beginning engineers. Entry-level jobs usually involve routine work, often as a member of a supervised team. After a year or more (depending on job performance and qualifications), one becomes a junior engineer, then an assistant to perhaps one or more supervising engineers. Establishment as a professional engineer comes after passing the PE exam.

ADVANCEMENT

Professional engineers with many years' experience often join with partners to establish their own firms in design, consulting, or contracting. Some leave long-held positions to be assigned as top executives in industries such as manufacturing and business consulting. Also, there are those who return to academia to teach high school or college students. For all of these potential opportunities, it is necessary to keep abreast of engineering advancements and trends by reading industry journals and taking courses.

EARNINGS

Civil engineers are among the lowest paid in the engineering field; however, their salaries are high when compared to those of many other occupations. The median annual earnings for civil engineers were $74,600 in 2008, according to the U.S. Department of Labor. The lowest paid 10 percent made less than $48,140 per year, and, at the other end of the pay scale, 10 percent earned more than $115,630 annually.

Civil engineers working for the federal government had a mean salary of $85,970 in 2008. According to a 2007 survey by the National Association of Colleges and Employers (the most recent survey available), starting salaries for civil engineers by degree level averaged as follows: bachelor's, $48,509; master's, $48,280; and doctorate, $62,275. As with all occupations, salaries are higher for those with more experience. Top civil engineers earn more than $120,000 a year.

Benefits typically include such extras as health insurance, retirement plans, and paid vacation days.

WORK ENVIRONMENT

Many civil engineers work regular 40-hour weeks, often in or near major industrial and commercial areas. Sometimes they are assigned to work in remote areas and foreign countries. Because of the diversity of civil engineering positions, working conditions vary widely. Offices, labs, factories, and actual sites are typical environments for engineers.

A typical work cycle involving various types of civil engineers involves three stages: planning, constructing, and maintaining. Those involved with development of a campus compound, for example, would first need to work in their offices developing plans for a survey. Surveying and mapping engineers would have to visit the proposed site to take measurements and perhaps shoot aerial photographs. The measurements and photos would have to be converted into drawings and blueprints. Geotechnical engineers would dig wells at the site and take core samples from the ground. If toxic waste or unexpected water is found at the site, the contractor determines what should be done.

Actual construction then begins. Very often, a field trailer on the site becomes the engineers' makeshift offices. The campus might take several years to build—it is not uncommon for engineers to be involved in long-term projects. If contractors anticipate that deadlines will not be met, they often put in weeks of 10- to 15-hour days on the job.

After construction is complete, engineers spend less and less time at the site. Some may be assigned to stay on-site to keep daily surveys of how the structure is holding up and to solve problems when they arise. Eventually, the project engineers finish the job and move on to another long-term assignment.

OUTLOOK

Employment for civil engineers is expected to grow faster than the average for all occupations through 2018, according to the

U.S. Department of Labor. Employment will come from the need to maintain and repair public works, such as highways, bridges, and water systems. In addition, as the population grows, so does the need for more transportation and pollution control systems, which creates jobs for those who construct these systems. Firms providing management consulting and computer services may also be sources of jobs for civil engineers. However, employment is affected by several factors, including decisions made by the government to spend further on renewing and adding to the country's basic infrastructure and the health of the economy in general.

FOR MORE INFORMATION

For information on training and scholarships, and to read Career Paths in Civil Engineering, *visit the society's Web site.*
   American Society of Civil Engineers
   1801 Alexander Bell Drive
   Reston, VA 20191-4400
   Tel: 800-548-2723
   http://www.asce.org

For information on careers and colleges and universities with ITE student chapters, contact
   Institute of Transportation Engineers (ITE)
   1099 14th Street, NW, Suite 300 West
   Washington, DC 20005-3438
   Tel: 202-289-0222
   Email: ite_staff@ite.org
   http://www.ite.org

The JETS offers high school students the opportunity to try engineering through a number of programs and competitions. To find out more about these opportunities or for general career information, contact
   Junior Engineering Technical Society (JETS)
   1420 King Street, Suite 405
   Alexandria, VA 22314-2794
   Tel: 703-548-5387
   Email: info@jets.org
   http://www.jets.org

Construction Inspectors

QUICK FACTS

School Subjects
Mathematics
Technical/shop

Personal Skills
Leadership/management
Technical/scientific

Work Environment
Indoors and outdoors
Primarily multiple locations

Minimum Education Level
High school diploma

Salary Range
$31,270 to $50,180 to
$78,070

Certification or Licensing
Required by certain states

Outlook
Faster than the average

DOT
182

GOE
02.08.02

NOC
2264

O*NET-SOC
47-4011.00

OVERVIEW

Construction inspectors work for federal, state, and local governments. Their job is to examine the construction, alteration, or repair of highways, streets, sewer and water systems, dams, bridges, buildings, and other structures to ensure that they comply with building codes and ordinances, zoning regulations, and contract specifications. Approximately 106,400 construction and building inspectors work in the United States.

HISTORY

Construction is one of the major industries of the modern world. Public construction includes structures such as public housing projects, schools, hospitals, administrative and service buildings, industrial and military facilities, highways, and sewer and water systems.

To ensure the public safety of these structures and systems, various governing bodies establish building codes that contractors must follow. It is the job of the construction inspector to ensure that the codes are properly followed.

THE JOB

This occupation is made up of four broad categories of specialization: building, electrical, mechanical, and public works.

Building inspectors examine the structural quality of buildings. They check the plans before construction, visit the work site a number of times during construction, and make a final inspection when the project is completed. Some building inspectors specialize in areas such as structural steel or reinforced concrete buildings.

Electrical inspectors visit work sites to inspect the installation of electrical systems and equipment. They check wiring, lighting, generators, and sound and security systems. They may also inspect the wiring for elevators, heating and air-conditioning systems, kitchen appliances, and other electrical installations.

Mechanical inspectors inspect plumbing systems and the mechanical components of heating and air-conditioning equipment and kitchen appliances. They also examine gas tanks, piping, and gas-fired appliances. Some mechanical inspectors specialize in elevators, plumbing, or boilers.

Elevator inspectors inspect both the mechanical and the electrical features of lifting and conveying devices, such as elevators, escalators, and moving sidewalks. They also test their speed, load allowances, brakes, and safety devices.

Plumbing inspectors inspect plumbing installations, water supply systems, drainage and sewer systems, water heater installations, fire sprinkler systems, and air and gas piping systems; they also examine building sites for soil type to determine water table level, seepage rate, and similar conditions.

Heating and refrigeration inspectors examine heating, ventilating, air-conditioning, and refrigeration installations in new buildings and approve alteration plans for those elements in existing buildings.

Public works inspectors make sure that government construction of water and sewer systems, highways, streets, bridges, and dams conforms to contract specifications. They visit work sites to inspect excavations, mixing and pouring of concrete, and asphalt paving. They also keep records of the amount of work performed and the materials used so that proper payment can be made. These inspectors may specialize in highways, reinforced concrete, or ditches.

Construction inspectors use measuring devices and other test equipment, take photographs, keep a daily log of their work, and write reports. If any detail of a project does not comply with the various codes, ordinances, or specifications, or if construction is being done without proper permits, the inspectors have the authority to issue a stop-work order.

REQUIREMENTS

High School

People interested in becoming construction inspectors must be high school graduates who have taken courses in drafting, algebra, geometry, and English. Additional shop courses will undoubtedly prove helpful as well.

Postsecondary Training

Employers prefer graduates of an apprenticeship program, community or junior college, or people with at least two years toward an engineering or architectural degree. Required courses include construction technology, blueprint reading, technical math, English, and building inspection. Only 28 percent of construction and building inspectors had a bachelor's degree or higher in 2006, according to the U.S. Department of Labor.

Most construction inspectors have several years' experience either as a construction contractor or supervisor, or as a craft or trade worker such as a carpenter, electrician, plumber, or pipefitter. This experience demonstrates a knowledge of construction materials and practices, which is necessary in inspections. Construction inspectors receive most of their training on the job.

Certification or Licensing

Some states require certification for employment. Inspectors can earn a certificate by passing examinations on construction techniques, materials, and code requirements. The exams are offered by the International Code Council. The Association of Construction Inspectors, the International Association of Electrical Inspectors, NAESA International, and the National Association of Home Inspectors also offer certification designations. Contact these organizations for more information.

Other Requirements

A construction inspector should have experience in construction, have a good driving record, be in good physical shape, have good communication skills, be able to pay attention to details, and have a strong personality. Although there are no standard requirements to enter this occupation, an inspector should be a responsible individual with in-depth knowledge of the construction trades. Inexperience can lead to mistakes that can cost someone a staggering amount of money or even cause a person's death.

The trade is not considered hazardous, but most inspectors wear hard hats as a precaution. Inspectors might need to climb ladders and walk across rooftops or perhaps trudge up numerous flights of stairs at building projects where elevators are not yet installed. They might occasionally find themselves squirming through the dirty, narrow, spider-infested crawl space under a house to check a foundation or crawling across the joists in a cramped, dusty, unfinished attic, inhaling insulation fibers and pesticides.

After the inspection a construction inspector needs to explain his or her findings clearly in reports and should expect to spend many hours answering questions in person, by telephone, and in letters. Because they often deliver bad news, they also need the emotional strength to stand firm on their reports, even when someone calls them a liar or threatens to sue.

On the other hand, an inspector knows that their work is to protect people. For example, they help ensure that a couple's new house will not be apt to burn down from an electrical short, and they might point out less dangerous problems, such as a malfunctioning septic tank or a leaking roof, that could require expensive repairs.

EXPLORING

Field trips to construction sites and interviews with contractors or building trade officials are good ways to gain practical information about what it is like to work in the industry and how best to prepare for it. Summer jobs at a construction site provide an overview of the work involved in a building project. Students may also seek part-time jobs with a general contracting company, with a specialized contractor (such as a plumbing or electrical contractor), or as a carpenter's helper. Jobs in certain supply houses will help students become familiar with construction materials.

EMPLOYERS

Approximately 106,400 construction and building inspectors are employed in the United States. Approximately 44 percent work for local governments, such as municipal or county building departments. Another 27 percent work for architecture or engineering firms. Inspectors employed at the federal level work for such agencies as the Department of Defense or the Departments of Housing and Urban Development, Agriculture, and the Interior.

STARTING OUT

People without postsecondary education usually enter the construction industry as a trainee or apprentice. Graduates of technical schools or colleges of construction and engineering can expect to start work as an engineering aide, drafter, estimator, or assistant engineer. Jobs may be found through school career services offices, employment agencies, and unions or by applying directly to contracting company personnel offices. Application may also be made directly to the employment offices of the federal, state, or local governments.

Green Construction Resources

Books

Croston, Glenn. *75 Green Businesses You Can Start to Make Money and Make a Difference*. Newburgh, N.Y.: Entrepreneur Media Inc., 2008.

Earley, Sandra Leibowitz. *Ecological Design and Building Schools: Green Guide to Educational Opportunities in the United States and Canada*. Oakland, Calif.: New Village Press, 2005.

Freed, Eric Corey. *Green Building & Remodeling For Dummies*. Hoboken, N.J.: For Dummies, 2007.

Johnston, David, and Scott Gibson. *Green from the Ground Up: Sustainable, Healthy, and Energy-Efficient Home Construction*. Newtown, Conn.: The Taunton Press, 2008.

Llewellyn, A. Bronwyn. *Green Jobs: A Guide to Eco-Friendly Employment*. Cincinnati, Ohio: Adams Media, 2008.

McNamee, Gregory. *Careers in Renewable Energy: Get a Green Energy Job*. Masonville, Colo.: PixyJack Press, 2008.

Renner, Michael. *Green Jobs: Working for People and the Environment*. Washington, D.C.: Worldwatch Institute, 2008.

Yudelson, Jerry. *Green Building A to Z: Understanding the Language of Green Building*. Gabriola Island, B.C., Canada: New Society Publishers, 2007.

Web Sites

Green for All
http://www.greenforall.org

U.S. Department of Energy: Energy Efficiency and Renewable Energy
http://www.eere.energy.gov

U.S. Environmental Protection Agency
http://www.epa.gov/greenbuilding/pubs/about.htm#1

U.S. Green Building Council
http://www.usgbc.org

Whole Building Design Guide
http://www.wbdg.org

ADVANCEMENT

The federal, state, and large city governments provide formal training programs for their construction inspectors to keep them abreast of new building code developments and to broaden their knowledge of construction materials, practices, and inspection techniques.

Inspectors for small agencies can upgrade their skills by attending state-conducted training programs or taking college or correspondence courses. An engineering degree is usually required to become a supervisory inspector.

EARNINGS

The U.S. Department of Labor reports the median annual income for construction and building inspectors was $50,180 in 2008. The lowest paid 10 percent of these workers had annual earnings of less than $31,270; the highest paid 10 percent made more than $78,070. Earnings vary based on the inspector's experience, the type of employer, and the location of the work. Salaries are slightly higher in the North and West than in the South and are considerably higher in large metropolitan areas. Building inspectors earn slightly more than other inspectors.

Full-time construction and building inspectors usually receive paid vacations and holidays, sick leave, hospitalization and insurance benefits, and pension programs.

WORK ENVIRONMENT

Construction inspectors work both indoors and outdoors, dividing their time between their offices and the work sites. Inspection sites are dirty and cluttered with tools, machinery, and debris. Although the work is not considered hazardous, inspectors must climb ladders and stairs and crawl under buildings.

The hours are usually regular, but when there is an accident at a site, the inspector has to remain on the job until reports have been completed. The work is steady year-round, rather than the seasonal nature of some other construction occupations. In slow construction periods, the inspectors are kept busy examining the renovation of older buildings.

OUTLOOK

As the concern for public safety and an emphasis on green and sustainable design continues to increase, the demand for inspectors should grow faster than the average for all occupations through 2018, even if construction activity does not increase. The level of new construction fluctuates with the economy, but maintenance and renovation continue during the downswings, so inspectors are rarely laid off. Applicants who have a college education, are already certified inspectors, or who have experience as carpenters, electricians, or plumbers will have the best opportunities. Construction and building inspectors tend to be older, more experienced workers who have worked in other construction occupations for many years.

FOR MORE INFORMATION

For additional information on a career as a construction or home inspector, contact the following organizations:

American Construction Inspectors Association
530 South Lake Avenue, #431
Pasadena, CA 91101-3515
Tel: 888-867-2242
http://www.acia.com

American Society of Home Inspectors
932 Lee Street, Suite 101
Des Plaines, IL 60016-6546
Tel: 800-743-2744
http://www.ashi.com

Association of Construction Inspectors
21640 North 19th Avenue, Suite C-2
Phoenix, AZ 85027-2720
Tel: 623-580-4646
Email: info@aci-assoc.org
http://www.aci-assoc.org

International Association of Electrical Inspectors
901 Waterfall Way, Suite 602
Richardson, TX 75080-7702
Tel: 800-786-4234
http://www.iaei.org

International Code Council
500 New Jersey Avenue, NW, 6th Floor
Washington, DC 20001-2070
Tel: 888-422-7233
http://www.iccsafe.org

NAESA International
6957 Littlerock Road, SW, Suite A
Tumwater, WA 98512-7246
Tel: 360-292-4968

Email: info@naesai.org
http://www.naesai.org

National Association of Home Inspectors
4248 Park Glen Road
Minneapolis, MN 55416-4758
Tel: 800-448-3942
http://www.nahi.org

Construction Managers

QUICK FACTS

School Subjects
Business
Mathematics
Technical/shop

Personal Skills
Leadership/management
Technical/scientific

Work Environment
Indoors and outdoors
Primarily multiple locations

Minimum Education Level
Some postsecondary training

Salary Range
$47,000 to $79,860 to
$145,920

Certification or Licensing
Recommended

Outlook
Faster than the average

DOT
N/A

GOE
06.01.01

NOC
0711

O*NET-SOC
11-9021.00

OVERVIEW

Construction managers, also known as *construction foremen, supervisors,* and *contractors,* oversee the planning and building of residential, commercial, and industrial projects. They may be self-employed or salaried employees for large construction firms and real estate developers. Others may contract their services on a project-by-project basis. There are approximately 551,000 construction managers employed in the United States.

HISTORY

Construction, the building of any structure or infrastructure, has existed since early humans found the need to create shelter. Simple huts or cabins evolved to more sturdy structures, dirt paths changed to paved roads, and bridges were built to connect land once separated by rivers or streams.

As construction projects became larger and more complicated, the need arose for the construction manager: someone to organize and manage the many workers involved. In the past, managers came to their position after years of on-the-job experience—as carpenters, masonry workers, electricians, plumbers, or a host of other industry trades. Today, construction managers often have a college degree in construction science or engineering, as well as practical knowledge of the industry.

The growth of the construction industry and the need for qualified workers and managers resulted in the formation of various organizations devoted to training, educating, and advocating for those employed in construction. One such organization is the American Institute of Constructors (AIC). Incorporated in 1971, the AIC offers support and a standard of ethics for construction professionals. Members are entitled to continuing education and training, certification, and information on advances in the science of construction management.

THE JOB

The construction of any structure, whether a small bungalow or a skyscraper, is a complicated process. When erecting a new building, for example, an architect must first design the building according to the owner's wishes; carpenters, masonry workers, electricians, and plumbers must work on the foundation, interior, and exterior of the structure; and building inspectors must ensure all work is done according to the city's code. The construction manager is considered the supervisor and liaison for every step of a building's creation.

For smaller projects, such as a house, construction managers may be responsible for the entire project. If the house is to be built as part of a subdivision, they may act as a liaison between the developer and prospective homeowner. Construction managers may be asked to oversee any requested changes to the existing blueprint. They are also responsible for hiring and scheduling the various crews needed for construction—excavation teams to dig out and lay the foundation, carpenters for the frame and woodwork, masonry workers for exterior and interior brickwork, plumbers, electricians, and any specialized craftspeople needed to complete the project.

Industrial and large commercial projects are more complicated and may warrant more than one construction manager for the task. Assistant managers or foremen are often hired to oversee a particular part or phase of a large project, such as zoning and site preparation, or electrical and plumbing. Assistant managers may work with civil engineers on the structure of a new road, or with landscape architects on the renovation of a golf resort. Each assistant manager is responsible for applying for the necessary permits and licenses, as well as meeting with city code officers for periodic and final inspections. If the project does not pass inspection or violates any safety regulations, it is the manager's responsibility to bring the project to compliance.

Construction managers must know how to work within a budget. The inventory of building materials and tools is important. Managers must make sure costly supplies of steel and granite, for example, are not being wasted. They keep track of expensive tools and equipment and make certain they are used properly. If special equipment is needed, such as a state-of-the-art fire suppression system, construction managers must be able to procure it at a reasonable price.

The management of a large crew is a very important part of a construction manager's job. Once a qualified team of workers is assembled, their daily work output must be monitored, since it is the responsibility of the manager to make sure that a construction project is completed on schedule. Some managers may take on the responsibility of creating work schedules, calculating wages, or assigning benefits for workers. If there are any work-related issues, such as disagreements between workers, construction managers are called on to settle them. Most importantly, however, a construction manager is responsible for the safety of the crew and safe and timely completion of the final project.

REQUIREMENTS

High School
If you are thinking about a career in construction management, chances are you have a knack for building things. Industrial arts classes such as woodworking, welding, and drafting and design will give you good background experience for the construction industry.

Construction managers are savvy business professionals. Give yourself a solid introduction to the business side of this job by taking classes such as accounting, finance, management, and mathematics.

Postsecondary Training
Many construction managers have an associate's or bachelor's degree in construction science, construction management, or civil engineering. A typical class load for students studying construction science, for example, includes construction methods, building codes, engineering, site planning, and cost estimating. Some even earn their master's degree in these fields. Visit http://www.acce-hq.org for information on accredited programs.

Certification or Licensing
Certification is available from the AIC after successful completion of a written examination and verification of relevant work experience. Two designations are offered—associate constructor and certified professional constructor. Examinations cover different specialties

of the construction industry, including commercial, industrial, residential, mechanical, and electrical.

The Construction Management Association of America (CMAA) offers the designation of certified construction manager to applicants who pass an examination and meet educational and experience requirements. While AIC and CMAA certification programs are voluntary, many industry professionals choose to become certified, increasing their chances for promotion. Many employers look favorably upon job candidates with certification.

Other Requirements

Construction managers must have a thorough understanding of the construction business, ranging from the hands-on side to the managerial. They should be able to understand blueprints and technical drawings, and be familiar with the various tools and building materials. Some construction managers may use computer design programs to help with revising blueprints. Excellent supervisory skills are also needed to keep a project moving according to schedule, while at the same time motivating a crew to perform their best work.

Managers must be good communicators since they deal with many different types of people throughout the course of a building project, from engineers and city officials to trades people. Managers are often under great pressure to prepare contracts and bid on projects, as well as address any problems that arise during the project. For example, if a pre-ordered amount of steel is short of that needed to finish a structure, construction managers must be able to find more materials quickly, but without going beyond the project's budget.

EXPLORING

There are many ways to investigate this industry as a high school student. For example, you can try to find a part-time job at a local construction company. Don't count on operating the big machines—leave these to the professionals. Rather, you'll be given small tasks around the site, or assist trades people with their work. Regardless of the work, you can earn valuable experience and learn what the work environment is really like.

You can also manage your own building project, such as a tree house or fort. Enlist your friends to help you as designers or construction workers. You'll be in charge of completing each phase of the project—from designing the structure, setting the budget, ordering supplies, supervising your crew of workers, and building the structure.

Earnings for Construction Managers by Industry, 2008

Field	Mean Annual Earnings
Building equipment contractors	$81,590
Nonresidential building construction	$79,950
Other specialty trade contractors	$78,410
Foundation, structure, and building exterior contractors	$76,880
Residential building construction	$74,770

Source: U.S. Department of Labor

EMPLOYERS

Approximately 551,000 construction managers are employed in the United States. About 61 percent are self-employed. Employment opportunities exist in a variety of settings. Many construction managers work for small construction companies that specialize in residential homes or small commercial projects. They are often in charge of the entire project from start to finish.

Construction managers employed by larger firms, real estate developers, or engineering firms may only be assigned to work on a particular phase of the project, such as the structural framework, or specialize in a certain area such as fireproofing, or a specific type of construction such as bridges.

Jobs are located nationwide, but may be more plentiful in areas experiencing high growth. Managers who wish to work with larger companies and more visible projects may need to relocate to major metropolitan areas.

STARTING OUT

Traditionally, construction managers were promoted into managerial positions after many years of work experience in the construction industry. That is still possible today, though more common in smaller construction firms. Larger construction companies or major developers demand managerial candidates with construction experience as well as a college degree. Jobs can be found via school career services offices, newspaper and Internet job advertisements, employment agencies, and unions, or by applying directly to contracting company personnel offices. Professional organizations, such as the Construction Management Association of America, also list job listings at their Web sites.

ADVANCEMENT

Since construction managers already hold a high-tier position in the construction industry, promotion may be limited, especially with smaller firms. Some construction managers may move to larger companies that deal with bigger building contracts and projects. Promotion within larger companies may take the form of an upper-level management or executive position.

Some construction managers choose to open their own construction firms or branch off into real estate development. Others may choose to continue their education and become architects or engineers.

EARNINGS

Earnings for construction managers vary based on the manager's experience, the type of employer, and the location of the work. The U.S. Department of Labor reports the median annual income for construction managers was $79,860 in 2008. The lowest paid 10 percent of these workers had annual earnings of less than $47,000; the highest paid 10 percent made more than $145,920. Construction managers typically receive benefits such as health insurance, paid vacation and sick days, and eligibility for retirement savings plans.

WORK ENVIRONMENT

Construction managers work both indoors and outdoors. They typically work out of a central office, but spend a considerable amount of time at job sites. Although this career is not considered hazardous, job sites can be dirty and cluttered with tools, equipment, and construction debris.

Construction managers often travel between job sites that can be far apart. Some managers get the opportunity to oversee projects in other regions of the United States or even in other countries.

Managers work irregular hours and are often on call 24 hours a day to respond to emergencies, work stoppages due to weather delays, or to meet project deadlines.

OUTLOOK

Employment for construction managers is expected to grow faster than the average for all occupations through 2018, according to the U.S. Department of Labor. A shortage of qualified workers, the growing complexity and number of construction projects, and the need for better cost management of construction projects have spurred strong demand for construction managers—especially those with experience and bachelor's or higher degrees in construction science, construction management, or civil engineering.

FOR MORE INFORMATION

For information on accredited educational programs, contact
American Council for Construction Education
1717 North Loop 1604 E, Suite 320
San Antonio, TX 78232-1570
Tel: 210-495-6161
Email: acce@acce-hq.org
http://www.acce-hq.org

For industry news, student and full membership information, and certification opportunities, contact
American Institute of Constructors
PO Box 26334
Alexandria, VA 22314-6334
Tel: 703-683-4999
Email: admin@aicnet.org
http://www.aicnet.org

For information on different careers within the construction industry and apprenticeship information, contact
Building and Construction Trades Department, AFL-CIO
815 16th Street, Suite 600
Washington, DC 20006-4101
Tel: 202-347-1461
http://www.buildingtrades.org

For industry news and certification opportunities, contact
Construction Management Association of America
7926 Jones Branch Drive, Suite 800
McLean, VA 22102-3303
Tel: 703-356-2622

Email: info@cmaanet.org
http://cmaanet.org

To learn more about industry standards, available training programs, and career information, contact

National Center for Construction Education & Research
3600 NW 43rd Street, Building G
Gainesville, FL 32606-8134
Tel: 888-622-3720
http://www.nccer.org

INTERVIEW

Rebecca Mirsky is an associate professor and chair of the Construction Management program (http://coen.boisestate.edu/cm/home. asp) at Boise State University in Boise, Idaho. She has a Ph.D. in environmental engineering, is a licensed professional engineer, and is a Leadership in Energy and Environmental Design-accredited professional. Rebecca discussed the field with the editors of Careers in Focus: Construction.

Q. Can you please tell us about your program?
A. The Construction Management program at Boise State University is housed within the College of Engineering. We offer a four-year bachelor's degree in construction management accredited by the American Council for Construction Education. Our program has five full-time faculty.

Q. What is one thing that young people may not know about a career in construction management?
A. Construction management is a professional management degree made up of engineering, construction, and business courses. It is not a technical, craft, or trade program. And construction management is a great career for women!

Q. Green construction has been mentioned frequently in the news lately. Can you provide us with an overview of this specialty?
A. Green construction is a term used to describe construction materials and methods that result in buildings that use less energy, water, and resources; generate less waste; have less impact on the building site; and offer healthier indoor environments for the occupants. Green building is becoming more popular because people are realizing that we need to

protect our environment and our natural resources, be less wasteful, be more mindful of our energy and water use, and eliminate or limit harmful chemicals in our building materials. As more and more building owners demand healthier buildings, the construction industry is responding with greener building materials and methods.

Q. What advice would you give construction management students as they graduate and look for jobs?

A. Construction management is an exciting career for men and women. It requires a lot of teamwork, so employers are looking for applicants with excellent written and verbal communication skills, the ability to adapt quickly to a changing environment, creative problem-solving ability, and the desire to learn.

Q. What is the employment outlook for construction managers?

A. Prior to the current economic downturn, the Bureau of Labor Statistics was projecting that employment of construction managers would increase by 16 percent during the 2006–2016 decade, faster than average for all occupations. The current efforts to stimulate the economy are expected to provide a boost to construction employment, and the outlook is likely to improve more quickly than in other sectors. In other words, it is never a bad time to pursue a career in construction management!

Cost Estimators

OVERVIEW

Cost estimators use standard estimating techniques to calculate the cost of a construction or manufacturing project. They help contractors, owners, and project planners determine how much a project or product will cost to decide if it is economically viable. There are approximately 217,000 cost estimators employed in the United States.

HISTORY

Cost estimators collect and analyze information on various factors influencing costs, such as the labor, materials, and machinery needed for a particular project. Cost estimating became a profession as production techniques became more complex. Weighing the many costs involved in a construction or manufacturing project soon required specialized knowledge beyond the skills and training of the average builder or contractor. Today, cost estimators work in many industries but are predominantly employed in construction and manufacturing.

THE JOB

In the construction industry, the nature of the work is largely determined by the type and size of the project being estimated. For a large building project, for example, the estimator reviews architectural drawings and other bidding documents before any construction begins. The estimator then visits the potential construction site to collect information that may affect the way the structure is built, such as the site's access to transportation, water, electricity, and other needed resources. While out in the field, the estimator also analyzes the

QUICK FACTS

School Subjects
Business
Economics
Mathematics

Personal Skills
Leadership/management
Technical/scientific

Work Environment
Indoors and outdoors
Primarily multiple locations

Minimum Education Level
Some postsecondary training

Salary Range
$33,150 to $56,510 to $94,470+

Certification or Licensing
Recommended

Outlook
Much faster than the average

DOT
160

GOE
13.02.04

NOC
2234

O*NET-SOC
13-1051.00

topography of the land, taking note of its general characteristics, such as drainage areas and the location of trees and other vegetation. After compiling thorough research, the estimator writes a quantity survey, or takeoff. This is an itemized report of the quantity of materials and labor a firm will need for the proposed project.

Large projects often require several estimators, all of whom are specialists in a given area. For example, one estimator may assess the electrical costs of a project, while another concentrates on the transportation or insurance costs. In this case, it is the responsibility of a *chief estimator* to combine the reports and submit one development proposal.

In manufacturing, estimators work with engineers to review blueprints and other designs. They develop a list of the materials and labor needed for production. Aiming to control costs but maintain quality, estimators must weigh the option of producing parts in-house or purchasing them from other vendors. After this research, they write a report on the overall costs of manufacturing, taking into consideration influences such as improved employee learning curves, material waste, overhead, and the need to correct problems as manufacturing goes along.

To write their reports, estimators must know current prices for labor and materials and other factors that influence costs. They obtain this data through commercial price books, catalogs, and the Internet or by calling vendors directly to obtain quotes.

Estimators should also be able to compute and understand accounting and mathematical formulas in order to make their cost reports. Computer programs are frequently used to do the routine calculations, producing more accurate results and leaving the estimator with more time to analyze data.

REQUIREMENTS

High School
To prepare for a job in cost estimating, you should take courses in accounting, business, economics, and mathematics. Because a large part of this job involves comparing calculations, it is essential that you are comfortable and confident with your math skills. English courses with a heavy concentration in writing are also recommended to develop your communication skills. Cost estimators must be able to write clear and accurate reports of their analyses. Finally, drafting and shop courses are also useful since estimators must be able to review and understand blueprints and other design plans.

Postsecondary Training

Though not required for the job, most employers of cost estimators in both construction and manufacturing prefer applicants with formal education. In construction, cost estimators generally have associate's or bachelor's degrees in construction management, construction science, or building science. Those employed with manufacturers often have degrees in physical science, business, mathematics, operations research, statistics, engineering, economics, finance, or accounting.

Many colleges and universities offer courses in cost estimating as part of the curriculum for an associate's, bachelor's, or master's degree. These courses cover subjects such as cost estimating, cost control, project planning and management, and computer applications. The Association for the Advancement of Cost Engineering International offers a list of education programs related to cost engineering. Visit its Web site (http://www.aacei.org) for more information.

Certification or Licensing

Although it is not required, many cost estimators find it helpful to become certified to improve their standing within the professional community. Obtaining certification proves that the estimator has obtained adequate job training and education. Information on certification procedures is available from organizations such as the American Society of Professional Estimators, the Association for the Advancement of Cost Engineering International, and the Society of Cost Estimating and Analysis.

Other Requirements

To be a cost estimator, you should have strong mathematical and analytical skills. Cost estimators must work well with others and be confident and assertive when presenting findings to engineers, business owners, and design professionals. To work as a cost estimator in the construction industry, you will likely need some experience before you start, which can be gained through an internship or cooperative education program.

EXPLORING

Practical work experience is necessary to become a cost estimator. Consider taking a part-time position with a construction crew or manufacturing firm during your summer vacations. Because of more favorable working conditions, construction companies are the busiest during the summer months and may be looking for additional assistance. Join any business or manufacturing clubs that your school may offer.

Another way to discover more about career opportunities is simply by talking to a professional cost estimator. Ask your school counselor to help arrange an interview with an estimator to ask questions about his or her job demands, work environment, and personal opinion of the job.

EMPLOYERS

Approximately 217,000 cost estimators are employed in the United States: 59 percent by the construction industry and 15 percent by manufacturing companies (including those that manufacture electronics and computer products). Other employers include engineering and architecture firms, business services, the government, and a wide range of other industries.

Estimators are employed throughout the country, but the largest concentrations are found in cities or rapidly growing suburban areas. More job opportunities exist in or near large commercial or government centers.

STARTING OUT

Cost estimators often start out working in the industry as laborers, such as construction workers. After gaining experience and taking the necessary training courses, a worker may move into the more specialized role of estimator. Another possible route into cost estimating is through a formal training program, either through a professional organization that sponsors educational programs or through technical schools, community colleges, or universities. School career services counselors can be good sources of employment leads for recent graduates. Applying directly to manufacturers, construction firms, and government agencies is another way to find your first job.

Whether employed in construction or manufacturing, most cost estimators are provided with intensive on-the-job training. Generally, new hires work with experienced estimators to become familiar with the work involved. They develop skills in blueprint reading and learn construction specifications before accompanying estimators to the construction site. In time, new hires learn how to determine quantities and specifications from project designs and report appropriate material and labor costs.

ADVANCEMENT

Promotions for cost estimators are dependent on skill and experience. Advancement usually comes in the form of more responsibility and higher wages. A skilled cost estimator at a large construction company may become a chief estimator. Some experienced cost estimators go into consulting work, offering their services to government, construction, and manufacturing firms.

EARNINGS

Salaries vary according to the size of the construction or manufacturing firm and the experience and education of the worker. According to the U.S. Department of Labor, the median annual salary for cost estimators was $56,510 in 2008. The lowest paid 10 percent earned less than $33,150 and the highest paid 10 percent earned more than $94,470. By industry, the mean annual earnings were as follows: nonresidential building construction, $65,410; residential building construction, $55,390; building foundation, structure, and exterior contractors, $54,670; and building finishing contractors, $55,430. Starting salaries for graduates of engineering or construction management programs were higher than those with degrees in other fields. A salary survey by the National Association of Colleges and Employers reports that candidates with degrees in construction science/management were offered average starting salaries of $46,930 a year in 2007.

Benefits for full-time workers include vacation and sick time, health insurance, and pension or 401(k) plans.

WORK ENVIRONMENT

Much of the cost estimator's work takes place in a typical office setting with access to accounting records and other information. However, estimators must also visit construction sites or manufacturing facilities to inspect production procedures. These sites may be dirty, noisy, and potentially hazardous if the cost estimator is not equipped with proper protective gear such as a hard hat or earplugs. During a site visit, cost estimators consult with engineers, work supervisors, and other professionals involved in the production or manufacturing process.

Estimators usually work a 40-hour week, although longer hours may be required if a project faces a deadline. For construction estimators, overtime hours almost always occur in the summer when most projects are in full force.

OUTLOOK

Employment for cost estimators is expected to increase much faster than the average for all occupations through 2018, according to the

U.S. Department of Labor. As in most industries, highly trained college graduates and those with the most experience will have the best job prospects.

Many jobs will arise from the need to replace workers leaving the industry, either to retire or change jobs. In addition, growth within the residential and commercial construction industry is a large cause for much of the employment demand for estimators. The fastest growing areas in construction are in special trade and government projects, including the building and repairing of highways, streets, bridges, subway systems, airports, water and sewage systems, and electric power plants and transmission lines. Additionally, opportunities will be good in residential and school construction, as well as in the construction of nursing and extended care facilities. Cost estimators with degrees in construction management, construction science, or building science will have the best employment prospects in the construction industry.

FOR MORE INFORMATION

For information on certification and educational programs, contact
American Society of Professional Estimators
2525 Perimeter Place Drive, Suite 103
Nashville, TN 37214-3674
Tel: 888-EST-MATE
Email: SBO@aspenational.org
http://www.aspenational.org

For information on certification, educational programs, and scholarships, contact
Association for the Advancement of Cost Engineering International
209 Prairie Avenue, Suite 100
Morgantown, WV 26501-5934
Tel: 800-858-2678
Email: info@aacei.org
http://www.aacei.org

For information on certification, job listings, and a glossary of cost-estimating terms, visit the society's Web site.
Society of Cost Estimating and Analysis
527 Maple Avenue East, Suite 301
Vienna, VA 22180-4753
Tel: 703-938-5090
Email: scea@sceaonline.net
http://www.sceaonline.net

Drafters

OVERVIEW

Drafters prepare working plans and detailed drawings of products or structures from the rough sketches, specifications, and calculations of engineers, architects, and designers. These drawings are used in engineering or manufacturing processes to reproduce exactly the product or structure desired, according to the specified dimensions. The drafter uses knowledge of various machines, engineering practices, mathematics, and building materials, along with other physical sciences and fairly extensive computer skills, to complete the drawings. There are approximately 251,900 drafters working in the United States.

HISTORY

In industry, drafting is the conversion of ideas from people's minds to precise working specifications from which products can be made. Many people find it much easier to give visual rather than oral or written directions, and to assemble new equipment if the instructions include diagrams and drawings. This is especially true in complex situations or when a large number of people are involved; drawings allow all aspects to be addressed and everyone to receive the same information at the same time. Industry has come to rely on drafters to develop the working specifications from the new ideas and findings of people in laboratories, shops, factories, and design studios.

Until the 1970s drafting and designing were done with a pencil and paper on a drafting table. While some drafters still use pen-

QUICK FACTS

School Subjects
Art
Computer science
Mathematics

Personal Skills
Artistic
Technical/scientific

Work Environment
Primarily indoors
Primarily one location

Minimum Education Level
Some postsecondary training

Salary Range
$28,220 to $44,490 to
$67,110+

Certification or Licensing
Recommended (certification)
Required for certain positions (licensing)

Outlook
More slowly than the average

DOT
017

GOE
02.08.03

NOC
2253

O*NET-SOC
17-3011.00, 17-3011.01,
17-3011.02, 17-3012.00,
17-3012.01, 17-3012.02,
17-3013.00

cil and paper to create drawings, most use computer-aided design (CAD) and drafting technology. Today, there are tens of thousands of CAD workstations in industrial settings. CAD systems greatly speed up and simplify the designer's and drafter's work. They do more than just let the operator "draw" the technical illustration on the screen: They add the speed and power of computer processing, plus software with technical information that ease the designer/drafter's tasks. CAD systems make complex mathematical calculations, spot problems, offer advice, and provide a wide range of other assistance. Today, nearly all drafting tasks are done with such equipment.

As the Internet has developed, CAD operators can send a CAD drawing across the world in a matter of minutes attached to an email message. Gone are the days of rolling up a print and mailing it off via snail mail. Technology has once again made work more efficient for the CAD designer and drafter.

THE JOB

The drafter prepares detailed plans and specification drawings from the ideas, notes, or rough sketches of scientists, engineers, architects, and designers. Sometimes drawings are developed after a visit to a project in the field or as the result of a discussion with one or more people involved in the job. The drawings, which usually provide a number of different views of the object, must be exact and accurate. Such drawings usually include information concerning the quality of materials to be used, their cost, and the processes to be followed in carrying out the job. In developing drawings made to scale of the object to be built, most drafters use CAD systems. Technicians work at specially designed and equipped interactive computer graphics workstations. They call up computer files that hold data about a new product; they then run the programs to convert that information into diagrams and drawings of the product. These are displayed on a video display screen, which then acts as an electronic drawing board. Following the directions of an engineer or designer, the drafter enters changes to the product's design into the computer. The drafter merges these changes into the data file, and then displays the corrected diagrams and drawings.

The software in CAD systems is very helpful to the user—it offers suggestions and advice and even points out errors. The most important advantage of working with a CAD system is that it saves the drafter from the lengthy process of having to produce, by hand, the original and then the revised product drawings and diagrams.

The CAD workstation is equipped to allow drafters to perform calculations, develop simulations, and manipulate and modify the displayed material. Using typed commands at a keyboard, a stylus or light pen for touching the screen display, a mouse, joystick, or other electronic methods of interacting with the display, drafters can move, rotate, or zoom in on any aspect of the drawing on the screen, and project three-dimensional images from two-dimensional sketches. They can make experimental changes to the design and then run tests on the modified design to determine its qualities, such as weight, strength, flexibility, and the cost of materials that would be required. Compared to traditional drafting and design techniques, CAD offers virtually unlimited freedom to explore alternatives, and in far less time.

When the product design is completed and the necessary information is assembled in the computer files, drafters may store the newly developed data, output it on a printer, transfer it to another computer, or send it directly to another step of the automated testing or manufacturing process.

Drafters often are classified according to the type of work they do or their level of responsibility. Senior drafters use the preliminary information and ideas provided by engineers and architects to make design layouts. They may have the title of *chief drafter,* and so assign work to other drafters and supervise their activities. *Detailers* make complete drawings, giving dimensions, material, and any other necessary information of each part shown on the layout. *Checkers* carefully examine drawings to check for errors in computing or in recording dimensions and specifications.

Drafters also may specialize in a particular field of work, such as mechanical, electrical, electronic, aeronautical, structural, or architectural drafting. Although the nature of the work of drafters is not too different from one specialization to another, there is a considerable variation in the type of object with which they deal. The following paragraphs detail specialties in the construction industry and other fields.

Commercial drafters do all-around drafting, such as plans for building sites, layouts of offices and factories, and drawings of charts, forms, and records.

Civil drafters make construction drawings for roads and highways, river and harbor improvements, flood control, drainage, and other civil engineering projects. *Structural drafters* draw plans for bridge trusses, plate girders, roof trusses, trestle bridges, and other structures that use structural reinforcing steel, concrete, masonry, and other structural materials.

Cartographic drafters prepare maps of geographic areas to show natural and constructed features, political boundaries, and other features. *Topographical drafters* draft and correct maps from original sources, such as other maps, surveying notes, and aerial photographs. *Architectural drafters* draw plans of buildings, including artistic and structural features. *Landscape drafters* make detailed drawings from sketches furnished by landscape architects.

Heating and ventilating drafters draft plans for heating, air-conditioning, ventilating, and sometimes refrigeration equipment. *Plumbing drafters* draw diagrams for the installation of plumbing equipment. *Mechanical drafters* make working drawings of machinery, automobiles, power plants, or any mechanical device. *Castings drafters* prepare detailed drawings of castings, which are objects formed in a mold. *Tool design drafters* draft manufacturing plans for all kinds of tools. *Patent drafters* make drawings of mechanical devices for use by lawyers to obtain patent rights for their clients.

Electrical drafters make schematics and wiring diagrams to be used by construction crews working on equipment and wiring in power plants, communications centers, buildings, or electrical distribution systems. *Electronics drafters* draw schematics and wiring diagrams for television cameras and TV sets, radio transmitters and receivers, computers, radiation detectors, and other electronic equipment.

Electromechanisms design drafters draft designs of electromechanical equipment such as aircraft engines, data processing systems, gyroscopes, automatic materials handling and processing machinery, or biomedical equipment. *Electromechanical drafters* draw wiring diagrams, layouts, and mechanical details for the electrical components and systems of a mechanical process or device.

Aeronautical drafters prepare engineering drawings for planes, missiles, and spacecraft. *Automotive design drafters* and *automotive design layout drafters* both turn out working layouts and master drawings of components, assemblies, and systems of automobiles and other vehicles. Automotive design drafters make original designs from specifications, and automotive design layout drafters make drawings based on prior layouts or sketches. *Marine drafters* draft the structural and mechanical features of ships, docks, and marine buildings and equipment. Projects range from petroleum drilling platforms to nuclear submarines.

Geological drafters make diagrams and maps of geological formations and locations of mineral, oil, and gas deposits. *Geophysical drafters* draw maps and diagrams based on data from petroleum prospecting instruments such as seismographs, gravity meters, and magnetometers. *Directional survey drafters* plot bore holes for oil and gas wells. *Oil and gas drafters* draft plans for the construction and operation of oil fields, refineries, and pipeline systems.

A design team working on electrical or gas power plants and substations may be headed by a *chief design drafter,* who oversees architectural, electrical, mechanical, and structural drafters. *Estimators* and drafters draw specifications and instructions for installing voltage transformers, cables, and other electrical equipment that delivers electric power to consumers.

REQUIREMENTS

High School

If you are interested in a career as a drafter, begin your preparation in high school. Be sure to take many mathematics classes—especially algebra, geometry, and trigonometry. If your school offers courses in mechanical drawing, take as many as you can. If mechanical drawing is not available, take some art classes. Wood, metal, or electric shop may be helpful, depending on the field specialty in which you're interested. Geography or earth science courses are also useful. Enroll in any computer classes you can, especially those in computer-aided design; increased familiarity with technology will strengthen your job prospects.

Postsecondary Training

Preparation beyond high school (including courses in the physical sciences, mathematics, drawing, sketching and drafting techniques, and in other technical areas) is essential for certain types of beginning positions, as well as for advancement to positions of greater salary and more responsibility. This training is available through technical institutes, community colleges, and four-year colleges. However, the quality of programs varies greatly, so you should be careful about choosing one that meets your needs. Ask potential employers about their educational preferences, and check the qualifications of various schools' faculties. Generally, two-year community college programs that lead to an associate's degree offer a more well-rounded education than those provided by technical schools. Also, four-year colleges typically do not offer specific drafting training but have courses in areas such as engineering and architecture.

With respect to choosing a school for advanced training in drafting, exposure to CAD technology has become a necessity. Keep in mind, however, that CAD is a tool; it can help if manual drawing skill is not your strong suit. It does not replace knowledge and experience, or creativity and imagination. A thorough grounding in the traditional drawing methods of drafting is as vitally important today as facility with CAD.

Did You Know?

- Approximately 9.6 million people work in the construction industry. Twenty-four percent of workers are employed in residential and nonresidential construction.
- Women make up 10 percent of workers in the construction industry.
- There are about 883,000 construction establishments in the United States.
- About 20 percent of people in the construction industry work more than 45 hours a week.

Sources: *Career Guide to Industries*, National Center for Construction Education and Research

Certification or Licensing

Certification is not presently required but is recommended in this field. Employers often look for graduates whose skills have been approved by a reliable industry source. The American Design Drafting Association/American Digital Design Association (ADDA) offers certification; becoming certified will enhance your credibility as a professional and could give you an edge in the job market.

ADDA also certifies schools that offer a drafting curriculum. As with individual certification, this accreditation process is not yet mandatory (although it can be a help to applicants in choosing where they'd like to receive training). Increasingly, however, states have begun to require that schools be ADDA-accredited (in order to receive grant funding, for instance). This suggests that required certification, and perhaps licensing, may be on the horizon.

Licensing requirements vary. Licensing may be required for specific projects, such as a construction project, when the client requires it.

Other Requirements

Students interested in drafting should have a good sense of both spatial perception (the ability to visualize objects in two or three dimensions) and formal perception (the ability to compare and discriminate between shapes, lines, forms, and shadings). Good hand-eye coordination is also necessary for the fine detail work involved in drafting.

EXPLORING

High school programs provide several opportunities for gaining experience in drafting. Mechanical drawing and computer-aided design are good courses to take. There are also many hobbies and leisure activities, such as woodworking, building models, and repairing and remodeling projects, that require the preparation of drawings or use of blueprints. After the completion of some courses in mechanical drawing or computer-aided design, it may be possible to locate a part-time or summer job in drafting.

EMPLOYERS

Approximately 251,900 drafters are employed in the United States, with approximately 52 percent employed by architectural, engineering, and related services firms that design construction projects. Others work in manufacturing, in automotive or aerospace design, for heavy equipment manufacturers—almost anywhere where the end product must meet precise specifications. Other drafters work for transportation, communications, or utilities companies, or for local, state, or federal agencies. If a student has a particular interest in almost any field plus a desire to become a drafter, chances are good that he or she can find a job that will combine the two.

STARTING OUT

Beginning drafters generally have graduated from a postsecondary program at a technical institute or junior college. Skill certification through the American Design Drafting Association/American Digital Design Association may be advantageous. Applicants for government positions may need to take a civil service examination. Students with some formal postsecondary technical training often qualify for positions as *junior drafters* who revise detail drawings and then gradually assume drawing assignments of a more complex nature.

ADVANCEMENT

With additional experience and skill, beginning drafters become checkers, detailers, design drafters, or senior drafters. Movement from one to another of these job classifications is not restricted; each business modifies work assignments based on its own needs. Drafters often move into related positions. Some typical positions include technical report writers, sales engineers, engineering assistants, production foremen, and installation technicians.

EARNINGS

Earnings in this field are dependent on a number of factors, including skills and experience. Students with more extensive advanced training tend to earn higher beginning salaries. Salaries also are affected by regional demands in specific specialties, so where a drafter chooses to live and work will play a part in his or her salary. According to the U.S. Department of Labor, median annual earnings of architectural and civil drafters were $44,490 in 2008. Earnings ranged from less than $28,220 for the lowest paid 10 percent to more than $67,110 for the highest paid 10 percent. According to Salary.com, CAD drafters earned salaries that ranged from less than $30,768 to $52,456 or more in 2009.

Employers generally offer drafters a range of benefit options, including health insurance, retirement plans, and the like. Travel sometimes is considered an indirect benefit of a job. Although architects and engineers often travel to construction sites to inspect the development of individual projects, drafters seldom are required to travel. Construction drafters, for instance, may be asked to visit sites toward the end of construction to provide final drawings of the completed structure, but most of their work will be done from their offices.

WORK ENVIRONMENT

The drafter usually works in a well-lighted, air-conditioned, quiet room. This may be a central drafting room where drafters work side by side at large, tilted drawing tables or at CAD workstations. Some drafters work in an individual department, such as engineering, research, or development, where they work alone or with other drafters and with engineers, designers, or scientists. Occasionally, drafters may need to visit other departments or construction sites to consult with engineers or to gain firsthand information. But in general, this is a desk job.

Most drafters work a 40-hour week with little overtime. Drafters work at drawing tables or computer stations for long periods of time, doing work that requires undivided concentration, close visual work, and very precise and accurate computations and drawings. There is generally little pressure, but occasionally last-minute design changes or a rush order may create tension or require overtime.

OUTLOOK

The U.S. Department of Labor predicts that employment for drafters will grow more slowly than the average for all careers through 2018. Offshoring of CAD-related work may reduce employment opportunities for drafters. Increasing use of CAD technology will limit the demand for less skilled drafters, but industrial growth and more complex designs of new products and manufacturing processes will increase the demand for drafting services. In addition, drafters are beginning to do work traditionally performed by engineers and architects. Nevertheless, job openings will be available as drafters leave the field for other positions or retirement. Opportunities will be best for drafters who have at least two years of postsecondary training and have strong technical skills and significant experience using CAD systems. Employment trends for drafters do fluctuate with the economy, however. During recessions, fewer buildings and manufactured products are designed, which could reduce the need for drafters in architectural, engineering, and manufacturing firms.

FOR MORE INFORMATION

For information on careers in drafting and certification, contact
**American Design Drafting Association/American Digital
    Design Association**
105 East Main Street
Newbern, TN 38059-1526
Tel: 731-627-0802
Email: national@adda.org
http://www.adda.org

For news on laws affecting the field and other current topics, contact this union for the drafting community.
International Federation of Professional and Technical Engineers
501 3rd Street, NW, Suite 701
Washington, DC 20001-2760
Tel: 202-239-4880
http://www.ifpte.org

Drywall Installers and Finishers

QUICK FACTS

School Subjects
Mathematics
Technical/shop

Personal Skills
Following instructions
Mechanical/manipulative

Work Environment
Primarily indoors
Primarily multiple locations

Minimum Education Level
Some postsecondary training

Salary Range
$24,200 to $37,700 to
$65,980

Certification or Licensing
None available

Outlook
About as fast as the average

DOT
840

GOE
06.02.02

NOC
7284

O*NET-SOC
47-2081.00, 47-2081.02

OVERVIEW

Drywall installers and *drywall finishers* plan and carry out the installation of drywall panels on interior wall and ceiling surfaces of residential, commercial, and industrial buildings. There are approximately 237,700 drywall installers and finishers working in the United States.

HISTORY

Thousands of years ago people used trowel-like tools to plaster wet clay over the walls of crude shelters in an attempt to keep out the wind and the rain. When the Great Pyramid of Cheops was built nearly 4,500 years ago, the Egyptians used a gypsum plaster to decorate the surfaces of its interior passages and rooms. But gypsum plaster is difficult to work with, because it may harden before it can be properly applied. It was not until around 1900 that additives were used to control the setting time of gypsum, thus opening the door for modern plastering techniques and products.

Drywall panels consist of a thin layer of gypsum plaster between two sheets of heavy paper. Different thicknesses and kinds of covering on the drywall offer different levels of moisture resistance, fire resistance, and other characteristics. Today, drywall construction is used in most new and renovated buildings because drywall can be installed cheaply and quickly. The panels are easier to work with than traditional plaster, which must be applied wet and allowed to dry before work can proceed. The widespread use of drywall has created a need for workers who are skilled in its installation.

THE JOB

Drywall panels are manufactured in standard sizes, such as 4 feet by 12 feet or 4 feet by 8 feet. With such large sizes, the panels are heavy and awkward to handle and often must be cut into pieces. The pieces must be fitted together and applied over the entire surface of walls, ceilings, soffits, shafts, and partitions, including any odd-shaped and small areas, such as those above or below windows.

Installers, also called *framers* or *hangers,* begin by measuring the wall or ceiling areas and marking the drywall panels with chalk lines and markers. Using a straightedge and utility knife, they score the board along the cutting lines and break off the excess. With a keyhole saw, they cut openings for electrical outlets, vents, air-conditioning units, and plumbing fixtures. Then they fit the pieces into place. They may fasten the pieces directly to the building's inside frame with adhesives before they secure the drywall permanently with screws or nails.

Often the drywall is attached to a metal framework or furring grid that the drywall installers put up for support. When such a framework is used, installers must first study blueprints to plan the work procedures and determine which materials, tools, and assistance they will require. They measure, mark, and cut metal runners and studs and bolt them together to make floor-to-ceiling frames. Furring is anchored in the ceiling to form rectangular spaces for ceiling drywall panels. Then the drywall is fitted into place and screwed to the framework.

Since drywall is very heavy, drywall installers are often assisted by other workers. Large ceiling panels may have to be raised with a special lift. After the drywall is in place, drywall installers may measure, cut, assemble, and install prefabricated metal pieces around windows and doors and in other vulnerable places to protect drywall edges. They may also fit and hang doors and install door hardware such as locks, as well as decorative trim around windows, doorways, and vents.

Drywall finishers, or *tapers,* seal and conceal the joints where drywall panels come together and prepare the walls for painting or papering. Either by hand or with an electric mixer, they prepare a quick-drying sealing material called joint compound and then spread the paste into and over the joints with a special trowel or spatula. While the paste is still wet, the finishers press perforated paper tape over the joint and smooth it to embed it in the joint compound and cover the joint line. On large commercial projects, this pasting-and-taping operation is accomplished in one step with an automatic applicator. When the sealer is dry, the finishers spread another two coats of cementing material over the tape and blend it into the wall to conceal the joint. Any cracks, holes, or imperfections in the walls or ceiling are also filled with joint compound, and nail and screw heads are covered. After a final sanding of the patched areas, the surfaces are ready to be painted or papered. Drywall finishers may apply textured surfaces to walls and ceilings with trowels, brushes, rollers, or spray guns.

REQUIREMENTS

High School
Most employers prefer applicants who have completed high school, although some hire workers who are not graduates. High school courses in carpentry provide a good background, and mechanical drawing, blueprint reading, general shop, and mathematics classes, such as basic math and algebra, are also important.

Postsecondary Training
Many drywall installers and finishers are trained on the job, beginning as helpers who aid experienced workers. *Installer helpers* carry materials, hold panels, and clean up the job site. They learn how to measure, cut, and install panels. *Finisher helpers* tape joints and seal nail holes and scratches. In a short time, they learn to install corner guards and to conceal openings around pipes. After they have become skilled workers, both kinds of helpers complete their training by learning how to estimate the costs of installing and finishing drywall.

Other drywall workers learn the trade through apprenticeship programs, which combine classroom study with on-the-job training. A major union in this field, the United Brotherhood of Carpenters and Joiners of America, offers four-year apprenticeships in carpentry that include instruction in drywall installation. A similar four-year program for nonunion workers is conducted by local affiliates of the Associated Builders and Contractors and the National Association of Home Builders. The International Union of Painters and Allied Trades runs an apprenticeship for finishers.

Other Requirements
Since drywall installing and finishing is a construction job, employers prefer to hire candidates who are in good physical condition. You will need a certain amount of strength and endurance for this job. Also, good coordination is a must.

A drywall finisher uses a drywall tape applicator called a bazooka to tape joints and seams. (*David R. Frazier/The Image Works*)

EXPLORING

It may be possible for students to visit a job site and observe installers and finishers at work. Part-time or summer employment as a helper to drywall workers, carpenters, or painters or even as a laborer on a construction job is a good way to get some practical experience in this field.

EMPLOYERS

Approximately 237,700 drywall installers and finishers are employed in the United States. Roughly 19 percent of this number are self-employed. Most drywall installers and finishers work primarily for drywall contractors associated with the construction industry. Typically installers and finishers find work in more heavily popu-lated areas, such as cities, where there is enough work for full-time employment in their specialty.

STARTING OUT

If you want to work in this field, you can start out as an on-the-job trainee or as an apprentice. Those who plan to learn the trade as they work may apply directly to contracting companies for entry-level jobs as helpers. Good places to look for job openings include the offices of the state employment service, the classified ads section in local newspapers, and the local offices of the major unions in the field. Information about apprenticeship possibilities may be obtained from local contractors or local unions.

ADVANCEMENT

Opportunities for advancement are good for people who stay in the trade. Experienced workers who show leadership abilities and good judgment may be promoted to supervisors of work crews. Sometimes they become cost estimators for contractors. Other workers open their own drywall contracting business.

EARNINGS

The annual earnings of drywall workers vary widely. According to the U.S. Department of Labor, the median hourly wage of drywall installers was $18.12 in 2008. The lowest paid 10 percent earned less than $11.64, and the highest paid 10 percent earned more than $31.72. A full-time drywall installer could earn from $24,200 to $65,980 a year. Those workers who have managerial duties or their own business may make even more. Apprentices generally receive about half the rate earned by journeymen workers.

Some drywallers are paid according to the hours they work; others are paid based on how much work they complete. For example, a contractor might pay installers and finishers five to six cents for every square foot of panel installed. The average worker is capable of installing 35 to 40 panels a day, when each panel measures 4 feet by 12 feet.

Drywall workers usually work a standard workweek of 35 to 40 hours. Construction schedules sometimes require installers and finishers to work longer hours or during evenings or on weekends. Workers who are paid by the hour receive extra pay at these times.

Benefits for full-time workers include vacation and sick time and health and (sometimes) dental insurance. Self-employed drywall installers and finishers must provide their own benefits.

WORK ENVIRONMENT

Drywall installation and finishing can be strenuous work. The large panels are difficult to handle and frequently require more than one person to maneuver them into position. Workers must spend long hours on their feet, often bending and kneeling. To work high up on walls or on ceilings, workers must stand on stilts, ladders, or scaffolding, risking falls. Another possible hazard is injury from power tools such as saws and nailers. Because sanding creates a lot of dust, finishers wear protective masks and safety glasses.

Drywall installation and finishing is indoor work that can be done in any season of the year. Unlike workers in some construction occupations, drywall workers seldom lose time because of adverse weather conditions.

OUTLOOK

The U.S. Department of Labor predicts job growth for drywall installers and finishers to be about as fast as the average for all occupations through 2008. There should be plenty of opportunities, partly because of a lack of training programs available. Increases in new construction and remodeling and high turnover in this field means replacement workers are needed every year. In addition, drywall will continue to be used in many kinds of building construction, creating a demand for workers.

Jobs will be located throughout the country, although they will be more plentiful in metropolitan areas where contractors have enough business to hire full-time drywall workers. In small towns, carpenters often handle drywall installation, and painters may do finishing work. Like other construction trades workers, drywall installers and finishers may go through periods of unemployment or part-time employment when the local economy is in a downturn and construction activity slows.

FOR MORE INFORMATION

For an example of an apprenticeship program, check out the following Web site:
Arizona Carpenters Apprenticeship
http://www.azcarpenters.com

For information on the construction industry and educational opportunities, contact
Associated Builders and Contractors
4250 North Fairfax Drive, 9th Floor
Arlington, VA 22203-1607
Tel: 703-812-2000
Email: gotquestions@abc.org
http://www.abc.org

For information on state apprenticeship programs, visit
Employment & Training Administration
U.S. Department of Labor
http://www.doleta.gov

For career and training information for painters, drywall finishers, and others, contact
International Union of Painters and Allied Trades
1750 New York Avenue, NW
Washington, DC 20006-5301
Tel: 202-637-0740
Email: mail@iupat.org
http://www.iupat.org and http://www.finishingtradesinstitute.org

For information on union membership and apprenticeship programs, contact
United Brotherhood of Carpenters and Joiners of America
http://www.carpenters.org

Electricians

OVERVIEW

Electricians design, assemble, install, test, and repair electrical fixtures and wiring. They work on a wide range of electrical and data communications systems that provide light, heat, refrigeration, air-conditioning, power, and the ability to communicate. There are approximately 694,900 electricians working in the United States.

HISTORY

It was during the latter part of the 19th century that electric power entered everyday life. Before then, electricity was the subject of experimentation and theorizing, but had few practical applications. The widespread use of electricity was spurred by a combination of innovations—especially the discovery of a way to transmit power efficiently via overhead lines and the invention of the incandescent lamp, the telephone, and the electric telegraph. In the 1880s commercial supplies of electricity began to be available in some cities, and within a few years, electric power was transforming many homes and factories.

Today, electricians are responsible for establishing and maintaining vital links between power-generating plants and the many electrical and electronic systems that shape our lives. Along with the electricians who install and repair electrical systems for buildings, the field includes people who work on a wide array of telecommunications equipment, industrial machine-tool controls, marine facilities like ships and off-shore drilling rigs, and many other kinds of sophisticated equipment.

THE JOB

Many electricians specialize in either construction or maintenance work, although some work in both fields. Electricians in construction are usually employed by electrical contractors. Other *construction electricians* work for building contractors or industrial plants, public utilities, state highway commissions, or other large organizations that employ workers directly to build or remodel their properties. A few are self-employed.

When installing electrical systems, electricians may follow blueprints and specifications or they may be told verbally what is needed. They may prepare sketches showing the intended location of wiring and equipment. Once the plan is clear, they measure, cut, assemble, and install plastic-covered wire or electrical conduit, which is a tube or channel through which heavier grades of electrical wire or cable are run. They strip insulation from wires, splice and solder wires together, and tape or cap the ends. They attach cables and wiring to the incoming electrical service and to various fixtures and machines that use electricity. They install switches, circuit breakers, relays, transformers, grounding leads, signal devices, and other electrical components. After the installation is complete, construction electricians test circuits for continuity and safety, adjusting the setup as needed.

Maintenance electricians do many of the same kinds of tasks, but their activities are usually aimed at preventing trouble before it occurs. They periodically inspect equipment and carry out routine service procedures, often according to a predetermined schedule. They repair or replace worn or defective parts and keep management informed about the reliability of the electrical systems. If any breakdowns occur, maintenance electricians return the equipment to full functioning as soon as possible so that the expense and inconvenience are minimal.

Maintenance electricians, also known as *electrical repairers,* may work in large factories, office buildings, small plants, or wherever existing electrical facilities and machinery need regular servicing to keep them in good working order. Many maintenance electricians work in manufacturing industries, such as those that produce automobiles, aircraft, ships, steel, chemicals, and industrial machinery. Some are employed by hospitals, municipalities, housing complexes, or shopping centers to do maintenance, repair, and sometimes installation work. Some work for or operate businesses that contract to repair and update wiring in residences and commercial buildings.

A growing number of electricians are involved in activities other than constructing and maintaining electrical systems in buildings. Many are employed to install computer wiring and equipment, telephone wiring, or the coaxial and fiber optics cables used in telecommunications and computer equipment. Electricians also work in power plants, where electric power is generated; in machine shops, where electric motors are repaired and rebuilt; aboard ships, fixing communications and navigation systems; at locations that need large lighting and power installations, such as airports and mines; and in numerous other settings.

All electricians must work in conformity with the National Electrical Code as well as any current state and local building and electrical codes. (Electrical codes are standards that electrical systems must meet to ensure safe, reliable functioning.) In doing their work, electricians try to use materials efficiently, to plan for future access to the area for service and maintenance on the system, and to avoid hazardous and unsightly wiring arrangements, making their work as neat and orderly as possible.

Electricians use a variety of equipment ranging from simple hand tools such as screwdrivers, pliers, wrenches, and hacksaws to power tools such as drills, hydraulic benders for metal conduit, and electric soldering guns. They also use testing devices such as oscilloscopes, ammeters, and test lamps. Construction electricians often supply their own hand tools. Experienced workers may have hundreds of dollars invested in tools.

REQUIREMENTS

High School
If you are thinking of becoming an electrician, whether you intend to enter an apprenticeship or learn informally on the job, you should have a high school background that includes applied mathematics and science, shop classes that teach the use of various tools, and mechanical drawing. Electronics courses are especially important if you plan to become a maintenance electrician.

Postsecondary Training
Some electricians still learn their trade the same way electrical workers did many years ago—informally on the job while employed as helpers to skilled workers. Especially if that experience is supplemented with vocational or technical school courses, correspondence courses, or training received in the military, electrical helpers may in time become well-qualified crafts workers in some area of the field.

You should be aware, however, that most professionals believe that apprenticeship programs provide the best all-around training in this trade. Apprenticeships combine a series of planned, structured, supervised job experiences with classroom instruction in related subjects. Many programs are designed to give apprentices a variety of experiences by having them work for several electrical contractors doing different kinds of jobs. Typically, apprenticeships last four to five years and provides at least 144 hours of classroom instruction and 2,000 hours of on-the-job training each year. Completion of an apprenticeship is usually a significant advantage in getting the better jobs in the field.

Applicants for apprenticeships generally need to be high school graduates, at least 18 years of age, in good health, and with at least average physical strength. Although local requirements vary, many applicants are required to take tests to determine their aptitude for the work.

Most apprenticeship programs are developed and conducted by state and national contractor associations such as the Independent Electrical Contractors and the union locals of the International Brotherhood of Electrical Workers. Some programs are conducted as cooperative efforts between these groups and local community colleges and training organizations. In either situation, the apprenticeship program is usually managed by a training committee. An agreement regarding in-class and on-the-job training is usually established between the committee and each apprentice.

Certification or Licensing

Some states and municipalities require that electricians be licensed. To obtain a license, electricians usually must pass a written examination on electrical theory, National Electrical Code requirements, and local building and electrical codes. Electronics specialists receive certification training and testing through the International Society of Certified Electronic Technicians.

Other Requirements

You will need to have good color vision because electricians need to be able to distinguish color-coded wires. Agility and manual dexterity are also desirable characteristics, as are a sense of teamwork, an interest in working outdoors, and a love of working with your hands.

Electricians may or may not belong to a union. While many electricians belong to such organizations as the International Brotherhood of Electrical Workers; the International Union of Electronic, Electrical, Salaried, Machine, and Furniture Workers; Communications Workers of America; the International Association of Machinists and Aerospace Workers; and other unions, an increasing number of electricians are opting to affiliate with independent (nonunion) electrical contractors.

EXPLORING

Hobbies such as repairing radios, building electronics kits, or working with model electric trains will help you understand how electricians work. In addition to sampling related activities like these, you may benefit by arranging to talk with an electrician about his or her job. With the help of a teacher or guidance counselor, it may be possible to contact a local electrical contracting firm and locate someone willing to give an insider's description of the occupation.

EMPLOYERS

Approximately 694,900 electricians are employed in the United States. Electricians are employed in almost every industry imaginable, from construction (which employs 65 percent of wage and salary workers) to telecommunications to health care to transportation and more. Most work for contractors, but many work for institutional employers that require their own maintenance crews, or for government agencies. Approximately 9 percent of electricians are self-employed.

STARTING OUT

People seeking to enter this field may either begin working as helpers or they may enter an apprenticeship program. Leads for helper jobs may be located by contacting electrical contractors directly or by checking with the local offices of the state employment service or in newspaper classified advertising sections. Students in trade and vocational programs may be able to find job openings through the career services office of their school.

If you are interested in an apprenticeship, you may start by contacting the local union of the International Brotherhood of Electrical Workers, the local chapter of Independent Electrical Contractors, or the local apprenticeship training committee. Information on apprenticeship possibilities also can be obtained through the state employment service.

ADVANCEMENT

The advancement possibilities for skilled, experienced electricians depend partly on their field of activity. Those who work in construction may become supervisors, job site superintendents, or estimators for electrical contractors. Some electricians are able to establish their own contracting businesses, although in many areas contractors must obtain a special license. Another possibility for some electricians is to move, for example, from construction to maintenance work, or into jobs in the shipbuilding, automobile, or aircraft industry.

Many electricians find that after they are working in the field, they still need to take courses to keep abreast of new developments. Unions and employers may sponsor classes introducing new methods and materials or explaining changes in electrical code requirements. By taking skill-improvement courses, electricians may also improve their chances for advancement to better-paying positions.

EARNINGS

Most established, full-time electricians working for contractors average earnings about $21 per hour, or $43,680 per year for full-time work, according to the National Joint Apprenticeship Training Committee—and it is possible to make much more. According to the U.S. Department of Labor, median hourly earnings of electricians were $22.32 in 2008 ($46,420 annually). Wages ranged from less than $13.54 an hour for the lowest paid 10 percent to more than $38.18 an hour for the highest paid 10 percent, or from $28,160 to $79,420 yearly for full-time work. Beginning apprentices earn 40 to 50 percent of the base electrician's wage and receive periodic increases each year of their apprenticeship.

Overall, it's important to realize these wages can vary widely, depending on a number of factors, including geographic location, the industry in which an electrician works, prevailing economic conditions, union membership, and others. Wage rates for many electricians are set by contract agreements between unions and employers. In general, electricians working in cities tend to be better paid than those in other areas. Those working as telecommunications or residential specialists tend to make slightly less than those working as linemen or wiremen.

Electricians who are members of the International Brotherhood of Electrical Workers, the industry's labor union, are entitled to benefits including paid vacation days and holidays, health insurance, pensions to help with retirement savings, supplemental unemployment compensation plans, and so forth.

WORK ENVIRONMENT

Although electricians may work for the same contractor for many years, they work on different projects and at different work sites. In a single year they may install wiring in a new housing project, rewire a factory, or install computer or telecommunications wiring in an office, for instance. Electricians usually work indoors, although some must do tasks outdoors or in buildings that are still under construction. The standard workweek is approximately 40 hours. In many jobs, overtime may be required. Maintenance electricians often have to work some weekend, holiday, or night hours because they must service equipment that operates all the time.

Electricians often spend long periods on their feet, sometimes on ladders or scaffolds or in awkward or uncomfortable places. The work can be strenuous. Electricians may have to put up with noise and dirt on the job. They may risk injuries such as falls off ladders, electrical shocks, and cuts and bruises. By following established safety practices, most of these hazards can be avoided.

OUTLOOK

Employment of electricians will grow about as fast as the average for all occupations through 2018, according to the U.S. Department of Labor. Growth will result from an overall increase in both residential and commercial construction, as well as in power plant construction. In addition, growth will be driven by the ever-expanding use of electrical and electronic devices and equipment. Electricians will be called on to upgrade old wiring and to install and maintain more extensive wiring systems than have been necessary in the past. In particular, the use of sophisticated computer, telecommunications, and data-processing equipment and automated manufacturing systems is expected to lead to job opportunities for electricians. Electricians with experience in a wide variety of skills—including voice, data, and video wiring—will have the best employment options.

In addition to opportunities created by growth in the construction and residential industries and other fields, a large number of job openings will occur as a result of workers retiring or leaving the field for other occupations.

While the overall outlook for this occupational field is good, the availability of jobs will vary over time and from place to place. Construction activity fluctuates depending on the state of the local and national economy. Thus, during economic slowdowns, opportunities for construction electricians may not be plentiful. People working in this field need to be prepared for periods of unemployment between construction projects. Openings for apprentices also decline during economic downturns. Maintenance electricians are usually less vulnerable to periodic unemployment because they are more likely to work for one employer that needs electrical services on a steady basis. But if they work in an industry where the economy causes big fluctuations in the level of activity—such as automobile manufacturing—they may be laid off during recessions.

FOR MORE INFORMATION

For information on careers, visit
ElectrifyingCareers.com
http://www.electrifyingcareers.com

For information on state apprenticeship programs, visit
Employment & Training Administration
U.S. Department of Labor
http://www.doleta.gov

For more information about the industry, contact
Independent Electrical Contractors
4401 Ford Avenue, Suite 1100
Alexandria, VA 22302-1464
Tel: 703-549-7351
Email: info@ieci.org
http://www.ieci.org

For information about the rules and benefits of joining a labor union, contact
International Brotherhood of Electrical Workers
900 Seventh Street, NW
Washington, DC 20001-3886
Tel: 202-833-7000
http://www.ibew.org

For information on certification, contact
International Society of Certified Electronic Technicians
3608 Pershing Avenue
Fort Worth, TX 76107-4527
Tel: 800-946-0201
Email: info@iscet.org
http://www.iscet.org

For industry information, contact
National Electrical Contractors Association
Three Bethesda Metro Center, Suite 1100
Bethesda, MD 20814-6302
Tel: 301-657-3110
http://www.necanet.org

For background information on apprenticeship and training pro-grams aimed at union workers, contact

National Joint Apprenticeship and Training Committee
301 Prince George's Boulevard, Suite D
Upper Marlboro, MD 20774-7401
Email: office@njatc.org
http://www.njatc.org

Floor Covering Installers

OVERVIEW

Floor covering installers include a wide range of construction workers, each specializing in the materials with which they work. *Resilient floor layers* install, replace, and repair shock-absorbing, sound-deadening, or decorative floor covering such as vinyl tile and sheet vinyl on finished interior floors of buildings. *Carpet layers* install carpets and rugs, most often wall-to-wall carpeting. Approximately 160,500 floor covering installers are employed in the United States.

HISTORY

Around 1840 Erastus Bigelow, an American industrialist, developed a power carpet loom, the first in a series of machines that revolutionized carpet manufacturing. Bigelow's invention made possible the production of large quantities of attractive carpeting at reasonable prices. Now, wall-to-wall carpeting has become a standard covering for floors in middle-class homes and businesses.

Another flooring developed during the same era was linoleum. Patented in 1863, it was an inexpensive and durable flooring composed of linseed oil, powdered cork, and other materials on a fiber backing. An early kind of linoleum, called battleship linoleum, was first used on the decks of warships.

Many floor coverings today are made of materials that have been developed since World War II. The synthetic fibers often found in carpets today have significant practical advantages over the natural fibers used many years ago. Over the years, various materials have been used in resilient flooring, including rubber, asphalt, and cork. Newer resilient flooring is most often made of vinyl, a synthetic plastic material, or linoleum.

With the growing popularity of flooring materials like these came the need for skilled workers who could efficiently measure, cut, and install the materials to fit exactly, stay in place, and present a clean appearance. Today, floor covering installation is a well-established craft in the building trades.

THE JOB

Installers' tasks vary according to whether they specialize in the installation of carpets or resilient floor coverings. Some workers install both types of coverings. For any type, the preparation of the subfloor, the surface beneath the finish material, is very important. The subfloor surface must be firm, dry, smooth, and free of loose dust and dirt. Installers may have to sweep, scrape, sand, or chip dirt and other irregularities from the floor, as well as fill cracks with a filler material. Sometimes a new surface of plywood or cement must be laid down before any floor covering can be installed.

Experienced installers must be able to gauge the moisture content of the subfloor and decide whether conditions are suitable for installing the covering. They should also know about the various adhesives that can be used, depending on conditions. Once the subfloor surface is prepared, installers consult blueprints or sketches and carefully measure the floor to determine where joints and seams will fall.

When the layout is clear, the installers, often with the help of apprentices or assistants, measure and cut the covering to create sections of the proper size. They also cut and lay foundation materials such as felt on the subfloor. With chalk lines and dividers, installers lay out lines on the foundation material to guide them in installing the floor covering. They trowel on adhesive cement and lay the floor covering in place, following the guidelines. Installers must be especially careful to align the pieces if there is any pattern in the flooring. They must also pay particular attention to fitting the pieces in odd-shaped areas around door openings, pipes, and posts. To make tight seams where sections of sheet covering must join, they overlap edges and cut through both layers with a knife. After the covering is laid in place, they often run a roller over it to smooth it and ensure good adhesion.

When installing wall-to-wall carpeting, carpet layers measure the floor and plan the layout. They allow for expected foot-traffic patterns so that the best appearance and longest wear will be obtained from the carpet. They also must place seams where they will be least noticed.

Installers must make sure that the floor surface is in the proper condition and correct any imperfections that may show through the carpet. Some carpet can be tacked directly to certain kinds of floor, but in many buildings, including most residences, installers often use a tackless method of laying carpet. A tackless strip is a thin strip of plywood with rows of steel pins projecting upward from it to grip carpeting firmly in place. Installers nail tackless strips around the border of the floor. Next, they cut and place padding in the open area of the floor.

Carpet often comes in 12-foot sections, so larger rooms require sections of carpet to be seamed together. They may sew the seam with a curved needle and special thread or use a heat-activated adhesive tape and an electric heating tool, like an iron.

When pieces are cut and ready, installers position the carpet and stretch it with special tools so it fits evenly on the floor, without lumps or rolls. They fasten it in place and any excess material is trimmed off so that the carpet meets the wall and door thresholds with a snug, exact fit.

Carpet installers use hand tools, including mallets, staple guns, pry bars, trowels, carpet knives, and shears; measuring and marking devices, such as tape measures, straightedges, and chalk lines; and power tools, such as stretchers.

REQUIREMENTS

High School
High school courses that would provide you with a good background for floor covering include wood and metal shop classes, mechanical drawing, general mathematics, and geometry.

Postsecondary Training
Most installers gain their training as helpers working for flooring installation contractors and learn informally on the job. When they are first hired, helpers are assigned simple tasks, such as tacking down strips. As they gain skills and experience, they are given more difficult work, such as measuring and cutting. It may take an installer 18 months to two years of informal on-the-job training to learn the basics of carpet laying or resilient floor laying.

Apprenticeship programs, which often last three to four years, usually provide much more complete training in all phases of installation. Some apprenticeships teach installation of both types of flooring, while others specialize in just one covering. Apprentices

A carpet installer cuts a piece of carpeting. (*Jeff Greenberg/The Image Works*)

work under the supervision of experienced installers and typically attend classes in related subjects once a week.

Other Requirements
Employers look for applicants who have good manual dexterity and hand-eye coordination. Because installers work on the premises of the customer, they should also have a neat appearance and a courteous manner.

EXPLORING

A part-time or summer job as a helper working for a flooring installation contractor is the best way to gain experience and might even lead you to full-time employment later. Taking part in a home improvement project, such as installing vinyl floor tiles, would also provide an opportunity to try out the work.

EMPLOYERS

There are approximately 160,500 floor covering installers employed in the United States. About 35 percent of all installers are self-employed. Others work for contractors, many of which now specialize in carpet alone. Experienced installers may work for floor covering manufacturers or retailers, either as installers or as sales representatives.

STARTING OUT

After gaining experience as a helper and learning skills on the job, you can apply directly to floor covering contractors and retailers. For specific job leads, you could check the listings in newspaper classified ads or the local offices of the state employment service. Information on apprenticeships in the area may be available from contractors, the state employment service, or the local offices of unions to which some installers belong, such as the United Brotherhood of Carpenters and Joiners of America and the International Union of Painters and Allied Trades.

ADVANCEMENT

Installers who work for large floor-laying firms may be promoted to supervisor positions. Installers who are familiar with the business and can communicate effectively can move into sales jobs with retailers of flooring products. They could also become *cost estimators*—workers who measure floors, compute areas, and figure costs using their knowledge of the materials and labor required for various kinds of installations.

With experience and a client base, many installers decide to go into business for themselves as independent subcontractors.

EARNINGS

The earnings of floor covering installers vary depending on experience, geographic location, and whether wages are set by union contracts. Most installers are paid by the hour, but some are paid by the number of yards of flooring they install, a system that can benefit installers who work particularly fast.

According to the U.S. Department of Labor, carpet installers earned hourly salaries that ranged from less than $10.23 to $34.10 or more in 2008. They earned a median hourly salary of $17.80. Floor layers, except carpet, wood, and hard tiles earned hourly salaries that ranged from less than $10.55 to more than $30.84. Beginning workers such as apprentices and assistants usually make half of what an experienced installer earns. Their wages increase as they gain on-the-job training.

Floor covering installers who work for a company usually receive benefits such as vacation days, sick leave, health and life insurance, and a savings and pension program. Self-employed workers must provide their own benefits.

WORK ENVIRONMENT

Although floor covering installers usually work in the daytime, some work is done at night or on weekends to minimize disruption, such

Facts About the Carpet Industry

- In 2007 total industry shipments were 1.6 billion square yards.
- Seventy-four percent of carpet produced in the United States is installed in residential settings; the rest is installed in commercial buildings.
- Ninety percent of U.S. carpet is manufactured in the state of Georgia, which has 174 manufacturing plants.
- Carpet recycling measures keep about 200 million pounds of waste from entering landfills in the United States each year.

Source: The Carpet and Rug Institute

as work done in offices and stores. The standard workweek is 35–40 hours. Installers usually receive overtime for weekend and holiday work. Self-employed installers may work very irregular hours.

Floor covering installation involves fewer hazards than other construction trades. The areas where installers work are usually indoors, well lighted, clean, and comfortable. However, they must have good physical endurance to do the bending, reaching, and stretching that are involved with the job. Installers may suffer knee and back injuries from constantly kneeling as they work and lifting heavy rolls of floor covering.

OUTLOOK

Employment of all floor covering installers is expected to grow about as fast as the average for all occupations through 2018, according to the *Occupational Outlook Handbook*. Little or no growth is expected for carpet installers as more homeowners and businesses choose to install hardwood floors. Employment for workers who install laminate, cork, rubber, and vinyl should also have little or no growth as the popularity of these flooring materials decreases. Tile and marble setters should have the best employment opportunities in the next several years due to the increasing popularity of tile in shopping malls, hospitals, schools, restaurants, and upscale homes. (See the article "Marble Setters, Tile Setters, and Terrazzo Workers" for more information on this career.) Many job opportunities for floor covering installers will occur when experienced workers leave the field for other occupations or retire.

However, even during economic downturns, when new construction levels drop drastically, the need to renovate existing buildings will make employment opportunities available to installers.

FOR MORE INFORMATION

For additional industry and career information, contact
The Carpet and Rug Institute
PO Box 2048
Dalton, GA 30722-2048
Tel: 800-882-8846
http://www.carpet-rug.org

To read excerpts from Floor Focus *magazine, visit the following Web site:*
Floor Daily
http://www.floordaily.net

For information on the professional, educational, and other benefits of membership, contact
The Flooring Contractors Association
7439 Millwood Drive
West Bloomfield, MI 48322-1234
Tel: 248-661-5015
http://www.fcica.com

For industry information, contact
National Tile Contractors Association
PO Box 13629
Jackson, MS 39236-3629
Tel: 601-939-2071
http://www.tile-assn.com

For information on union membership and apprenticeships, contact
United Brotherhood of Carpenters and Joiners of America
http://www.carpenters.org

The association's site has a consumer guide section with helpful information on different types of flooring. The flooring professionals section has information on training and the floor covering industry.
World Floor Covering Association
2211 East Howell Avenue
Anaheim, CA 92806-6009
Tel: 800-624-6880
Email: wfca@wfca.org
http://www.wfca.org

Heating and Cooling Technicians

OVERVIEW

Heating and cooling technicians work on systems that control the temperature, humidity, and air quality of enclosed environments. They help design, manufacture, install, and maintain climate-control equipment. They provide people with heating and air-conditioning in such structures as shops, hospitals, malls, theaters, factories, restaurants, offices, apartment buildings, and private homes. They may work to provide temperature-sensitive products such as computers, foods, medicines, and precision instruments with climate-controlled environments. They may also provide comfortable environments or refrigeration in such modes of transportation as ships, trucks, planes, and trains. There are approximately 308,200 heating and cooling technicians employed in the United States.

HISTORY

The modern heating industry got its start with the appearance of piped steam heating during the industrial revolution. Piped hot water heating replaced steam in the 1830s because of its improved comfort level and lower temperature requirement. Oil and coal heat in the late 19th and early 20th centuries have largely been superceded by today's natural gas and electric heating. In recent years, radiant heat and geothermal heating have become more important within the heating industry.

Cooling or air-conditioning mechanisms were virtually unknown until 1842, when Dr. John Gorrie invented a cold-air machine to relieve the suffering of yellow fever patients in a Florida hospital. Naturally occurring ice was relied upon for refrigeration until shortly after the Civil War, when a process to produce artificial ice was invented and put to use in the Southern states. The development of synthetic refrigerant gases in the early 20th century led to the widespread use of mechanical refrigeration by the 1930s and home air-conditioning by the 1950s.

Initially, the equipment for the limited capacity air-conditioning, refrigeration, and heating systems was simple, and the skills needed to maintain them were comparatively easy to learn. Most technicians for this early equipment were trained by manufacturers and distributors. But as the field has expanded and the equipment has become much more sophisticated, workers have had to pursue more specialized knowledge and skills.

THE JOB

Many industries today depend on carefully controlled temperature and humidity conditions while manufacturing, transporting, or storing their products. Many common foods are readily available only because of extensive refrigeration. Less obviously, numerous chemicals, drugs, explosives, oil, and other products must be produced using refrigeration processes. For example, some room-sized computer systems need to be kept at a certain temperature and humidity; spacecraft must be able to withstand great heat while exposed to the rays of the sun and great cold when the moon or Earth blocks the sun, and at the same time maintain a steady internal environment; the air in tractor-trailer cabs must be regulated so that truck drivers can spend long hours behind the wheel in maximum comfort and safety. Each of these applications represents a different segment of a large and very diverse industry.

Heating and cooling technicians may work in installation and maintenance (which includes service and repairs), sales, or manufacturing. The majority of technicians who work in installation and maintenance work for heating and cooling contractors; manufacturers of air-conditioning, refrigeration, and heating equipment; dealers and distributors; or utility companies.

Technicians who assemble and install air-conditioning, refrigeration, and heating systems and equipment work from blueprints. Experienced technicians read blueprints that show them how to assemble components and how the components should be installed into the structure. Because structure sizes and climate-control specifications vary, technicians have to pay close attention to blueprint details. While working from the blueprints, technicians use algebra and geometry to calculate the sizes and contours of ductwork as they assemble it.

Heating and cooling technicians work with a variety of hardware, tools, and components. For example, in joining pipes and ductwork for an air-conditioning system, technicians may use soldering, welding, or brazing equipment, as well as sleeves, couplings, and elbow joints. Technicians handle and assemble such components as motors, thermometers, burners, compressors, pumps, and fans. They must join these parts together when building climate-control units and then connect this equipment to the ductwork, refrigerant lines, and power source.

As a final step in assembly and installation, technicians run tests on equipment to ensure that it functions properly. If the equipment is malfunctioning, technicians must investigate in order to diagnose the problem and determine a solution. At this time, they adjust thermostats, reseal piping, and replace parts as needed. They retest the equipment to determine whether the problem has been remedied, and they continue to modify and test it until everything checks out as functioning properly.

Some technicians may specialize in only one type of cooling, heating, or refrigeration equipment. For example, *window air-conditioning unit installers and servicers* work on window units only. *Air-conditioning and refrigeration technicians* install and service central air-conditioning systems and a variety of refrigeration equipment. Air-conditioning installations may range from small wall units, either water- or air-cooled, to large central plant systems. Commercial refrigeration equipment may include display cases, walk-in coolers, and frozen-food units such as those in supermarkets, restaurants, and food processing plants.

Other technicians are *furnace installers,* also called *heating-equipment installers.* Following blueprints and other specifications, they install oil, gas, electric, solid fuel (such as coal), and multifuel heating systems. They move the new furnace into place and attach fuel supply lines, air ducts, pumps, and other components. Then they connect the electrical wiring and thermostatic controls and, finally, check the unit for proper operation.

Technicians who work in maintenance perform routine service to keep systems operating efficiently and respond to service calls for repairs. They perform tests and diagnose problems on equipment that has been installed in the past. They calibrate controls, add fluids, change parts, clean components, and test the system for proper operation. For example, in performing a routine service call on a furnace, technicians will adjust blowers and burners, replace filters, clean ducts, and check thermometers and other controls.

Technicians who maintain oil- and gas-burning equipment are called *oil-burner mechanics* and *gas-burner mechanics,* or *gas-appliance servicers.* They usually perform more extensive maintenance work during the warm weather, when the heating system can be shut down. During the summer, technicians replace oil and air filters; vacuum vents, ducts, and other parts that accumulate soot and ash; and adjust the burner so that it achieves maximum operating efficiency. Gas-burner mechanics may also repair other gas appliances such as cooking stoves, clothes dryers, water heaters, outdoor lights, and grills.

Other heating and cooling technicians who specialize in a limited range of equipment include evaporative cooler installers, hot-air furnace installers and repairers, solar-energy system installers and helpers, and air and hydronic balancing technicians, radiant heating installers, and geothermal heating and cooling technicians.

In their work on refrigerant lines and air ducts, heating and cooling technicians use a variety of hand and power tools, including hammers, wrenches, metal snips, electric drills, pipe cutters and benders, and acetylene torches. To check electrical circuits, burners, and other components, technicians work with volt-ohm meters, manometers, and other testing devices.

REQUIREMENTS

High School
In high school, students considering the heating and cooling field should take algebra, geometry, English composition, physics, computer applications and programming, and classes in industrial arts or shop. Helpful shop classes include mechanical drawing and blueprint reading, power and hand tools operations, and metalwork. Shop courses in electricity and electronics provide a strong introduction into understanding circuitry and wiring and teach students to read electrical diagrams. Classes in computer-aided design are also helpful, as are business courses.

Postsecondary Training
Although postsecondary training is not mandatory to become a heating, air-conditioning, and refrigeration technician, employers prefer to hire technicians who have training from a technical school, junior college, or apprenticeship program. Vocational-technical schools, private trade schools, and junior colleges offer both one- and two-

year programs. Graduates of two-year programs usually receive an associate's degree in science or in applied science. Certificates, rather than degrees, are awarded to those who complete one-year programs. Although no formal education is required, most employers prefer to hire graduates of two-year applications-oriented training programs. This kind of training includes a strong background in mathematical and engineering theory. However, the emphasis is on the practical uses of such theories, not on explorations of their origins and development, such as one finds in engineering programs.

Certification or Licensing

Technicians who handle refrigerants must receive approved refrigerant recovery certification, which is a requirement of the Environmental Protection Agency and requires passing a special examination.

Voluntary certification for various specialties is available through professional associations. The heating and cooling industry recently adopted a standard certification program for experienced technicians. The Air Conditioning Excellence program is available to both installation and service technicians and is offered by North American Technician Excellence. Technicians must take and pass a core exam (covering safety, tools, soft skills, principles of heat transfer, and electrical systems) and one specialty exam of their choice (covering installation, service, system components, regulations, codes and safety). The specialties available are air-conditioning, air distribution, air-to-air heat pumps, gas furnaces, oil furnaces, hydronics gas, hydronics oil, light commercial refrigeration, commercial refrigeration, and HVAC efficiency analyst (senior level). Additionally, the Refrigeration Service Engineers Society (http://www.rses.org), Refrigerating Engineers & Technicians Association (http://www.reta.com), and HVAC Excellence (http://www.hvacexcellence.org) offer certification.

In some areas of the field, for example, those who work with design and research engineers, certification is increasingly the norm and viewed as a basic indicator of competence. Even where there are no firm requirements, it generally is better to be qualified for whatever license or certification is available. Some states and localities may also require heating and cooling technicians to be licensed.

Other Requirements

Persons interested in the heating and cooling field need to have an aptitude for working with tools, manual dexterity and manipulation, and the desire to perform challenging work that requires a high level of competence and quality. Students who are interested in how things work, who enjoy taking things apart and putting them back together,

Did You Know?

- Approximately 54 percent of heating and cooling technicians work for plumbing, heating, and air-conditioning contractors.
- Heating and cooling technicians in Alaska, the District of Columbia, Massachusetts, Minnesota, and Illinois receive the highest pay.
- Approximately 15 percent of heating and cooling technicians are members of a union.
- Sixteen percent of heating and cooling technicians are self-employed.

Source: U.S. Department of Labor

and who enjoy troubleshooting for mechanical and electrical problems may enjoy a career in air-conditioning, refrigeration, and heating.

EXPLORING

A student trying to decide on a career in heating and cooling technology may have to base the choice on a variety of indirect evidence. Part-time or summer work is usually not available to high school students because of their lack of the necessary skills and knowledge. It may be possible, however, to arrange field trips to service shops, companies that develop and produce heating and cooling equipment, or other firms concerned with the environmental control field. Such visits can provide a firsthand overview of the day-to-day work. A visit with a local contractor or to a school that conducts a heating and cooling technology training program can also be very helpful.

EMPLOYERS

Approximately 308,200 heating and cooling technicians are employed in the United States. While most heating and cooling technicians work directly with the building, installation, and maintenance of equipment via heating and cooling firms, some technicians work in equipment sales. These technicians are usually employed by manufacturers or dealers and distributors and are hired to explain the equipment and its operation to prospective customers. These technicians must have a thorough knowledge of their products. They may explain newly developed equipment, ideas, and principles, or assist dealers and distributors in the layout and installation of unfamiliar components. Some technicians employed as sales representatives contact prospective buyers and help them plan air-conditioning, refrigeration, and heating systems. They help the client select appropriate equipment and estimate costs.

Other technicians work for manufacturers in engineering or research laboratories, performing many of the same assembling and testing duties as technicians who work for contractors. However, they perform these operations at the manufacturing site rather than traveling to work sites as most contractors' technicians do. Technicians aid engineers in research, equipment design, and equipment testing. Technicians in a research laboratory may plan the requirements for the various stages of fabricating, installing, and servicing climate-control and refrigeration systems; recommend appropriate equipment to meet specified needs; and calculate heating and cooling capacities of proposed equipment units. They also may conduct operational tests on experimental models and efficiency tests on new units coming off the production lines. They might also investigate the cause of breakdowns reported by customers, and determine the reasons and solutions.

Engineering-oriented technicians employed by manufacturers may perform tests on new equipment, or assist engineers in fundamental research and development, technical report writing, and application engineering. Other engineering technicians serve as *liaison representatives,* coordinating the design and production engineering for the development and manufacture of new products.

Technicians may also be employed by utility companies to help ensure that their customers' equipment is using energy efficiently and effectively. *Utility technicians,* often called *energy conservation technicians,* may conduct energy evaluations of customers' systems, compile energy surveys, and provide customer information.

Technicians may also work for consulting firms, such as engineering firms or building contractors who hire technicians to estimate costs, determine air-conditioning and heating load requirements, and prepare specifications for climate-control projects.

Some technicians also open up their own businesses, either as heating and cooling contractors or consultants specializing in sales, parts supply, service, and installation.

STARTING OUT

Many students in two-year programs work at a job related to their area of training during the summer between the first and second years. Employers may hire them on a part-time basis during the second year and make offers of full-time employment after graduation. Even if a job offer isn't a possibility, the employer may be aware of other companies that are hiring and help the student with suggestions and recommendations, provided the student's work record is good.

Some schools make work experience part of the curriculum, particularly during the latter part of their program. This is a valuable way for students to gain practical experience in conjunction with classroom work.

It is not unusual for graduates of two-year programs to receive several offers of employment, either from contacts they have made themselves or from companies that routinely recruit new graduates. Representatives of larger companies often schedule interview periods at schools with two-year air-conditioning, refrigeration, and heating technician programs. Other, usually smaller, prospective employers may contact specific faculty advisers who in turn make students aware of opportunities that arise.

In addition to using their schools' career services office, resourceful students can explore other leads by applying directly to local heating and cooling contractors; sales, installation, and service shops; or manufacturers of air-conditioning, refrigeration, and heating equipment. State employment offices may also post openings or provide job leads. Finally, student membership in the local chapter of a trade association, such as one of those listed at the end of this article, can result in good employment contacts.

ADVANCEMENT

There is such a wide range of positions within this field that workers who gain the necessary skills and experience have the flexibility to choose between many different options and types of positions. As employees gain on-the-job work experience, they may decide to specialize in a particular aspect or type of work. They may be able to be promoted into positions requiring more responsibilities and skills through experience and demonstrated proficiency, but in some cases additional training is required.

Many workers continue to take courses throughout their careers to upgrade their skills and to learn new techniques and methods used within the industry. Training can take the form of a class offered by a manufacturer regarding specific equipment or it may be a more extensive program resulting in certification for a specific area or procedure. Skill-improvement programs that offer advanced training in specialized areas are available through vocational-technical institutes and trade associations. Technicians with an interest in the engineering aspect of the industry may go back to school to get a bachelor of science degree in heating and cooling engineering or mechanical engineering.

Technicians increase their value to employers and themselves with continued training. For example, a technician employed by a manufacturer may progress to the position of sales manager, who acts as liaison with distributors and dealers, promoting and selling the manufacturer's products, or to field service representative, who solves unusual service problems of dealers and distributors in the area. Technicians working for dealers and distributors or contractors may advance to a service manager or supervisory position, overseeing other technicians who install and service equipment. Another possible specialization is mechanical design, which involves designing piping, ductwork, controls, and the distribution systems for consulting engineers, mechanical contractors, manufacturers, and distributors. Technicians who do installation and maintenance may decide to move into sales or work for the research and development department of a manufacturing company.

Some technicians also open up their own businesses, becoming heating and cooling contractors, consultants, self-employed service technicians, or specializing in sales and parts distribution.

EARNINGS

The earnings of heating and cooling technicians vary widely according to the level of training and experience, the nature of their work, type of employer, region of the country, and other factors. Heating and cooling technicians had median hourly earnings of $19.08 in 2008, according to the U.S. Department of Labor. The lowest paid 10 percent earned less than $12.19, while the top paid 10 percent earned more than $30.59.

Heating and cooling apprentices usually earn about 50 percent of the wage rate paid to experienced workers. This percentage rises as apprentices gain experience and skill training in the field.

Many employers offer medical insurance and paid vacation days, holidays, and sick days, although the actual benefits vary from employer to employer. Some companies also offer tuition assistance for additional training.

WORK ENVIRONMENT

The working conditions for heating and cooling technicians vary considerably depending on the area of the industry in which they work. For the most part, the hours are regular, although certain jobs in production may involve shift work, and service technicians may have to be on call some evenings and weekends to handle emergency repairs.

Technicians who are employed in installation and service may work in a variety of environments ranging from industrial plants to construction sites and can include both indoor and outdoor work. Technicians may encounter extremes in temperature when servicing outdoor and rooftop equipment and cramped quarters when servicing indoor commercial and industrial equipment. They often have to lift heavy objects as well as stoop, crawl, and crouch when making repairs and installations. Working conditions can include dirt, grease, noise, and safety hazards. Hazards include falls from rooftops or scaffolds, electric shocks, burns, and handling refrigerants and compressed gases. With proper precautions and safety measures, however, the risk from these hazards can be minimized.

Technicians who work in laboratories usually work in the research and development departments of a manufacturing firm or an industrial plant. Technicians employed by distributors, dealers, and consulting engineers usually work in an office or similar surroundings and are subject to the same benefits and conditions as other office workers. Some technicians, such as sales representatives or service managers, go out periodically to visit customers or installation and service sites.

Heating and cooling technicians work for a variety of companies and businesses. They may be employed by heating and cooling contractors, manufacturers of heating and cooling equipment, dealers and distributors, utility companies, or engineering consultants. Some large institutions such as hospitals, universities, factories, office complexes, and sports arenas employ technicians directly, maintaining their own climate-control staffs.

OUTLOOK

Employment in the heating and cooling field is expected to increase much faster than the average for all occupations through 2018, according to the U.S. Department of Labor. Excellent opportunities are expected for heating and cooling technicians who have completed a formal apprenticeship or received training from an accredited technical school. Some openings will occur when experienced workers retire or transfer to other work. Other openings will be generated because of a demand for new climate-control systems for residences and industrial and commercial users. In addition, many existing systems are being upgraded to provide more efficient use of energy and to provide benefits not originally built into the system. There is a growing emphasis on improving indoor air and making equipment more environmentally friendly. Systems that use chlorofluorocarbons (CFCs) need to be retrofitted or replaced with new equipment, since regulations banning CFC production became effective in 2000.

Comfort is only one of the major reasons for environmental control. Conditioned atmosphere is a necessity in any precision industry where temperature and humidity can affect fine tolerances. As products and processes become more complex and more highly automated, the need for closely controlled conditions becomes increasingly important. For example, electronics manufacturers must keep the air bone-dry for many parts of their production processes to prevent damage to parts and to maintain nonconductivity. Pharmaceutical and food manufacturers rely on pure, dirt-free air. High-speed multicolor printing requires temperature control of rollers and moisture control for the paper racing through the presses. There is every reason to expect that these and other sophisticated industries will rely more in the coming years on precision control of room conditions. The actual amount of industry growth for these applications will hinge on the overall health of the nation's economy and the rate of manufacturing.

Technicians who are involved in maintenance and repair are not as affected by the economy as workers in some other jobs. For example, in bad economic times a consumer may postpone building a new house or installing a new air-conditioning system, but hospitals, restaurants, technical industries, and public buildings will still require skilled technicians to maintain their climate-control systems. Technicians who are versed in more than one aspect of the job have greater job flexibility and can count on fairly steady work despite any fluctuations in the economy.

FOR MORE INFORMATION

For information on careers and educational programs, contact
Air Conditioning Contractors of America
2800 Shirlington Road, Suite 300
Arlington, VA 22206-3607
Tel: 703-575-4477
Email: info@acca.org
http://www.acca.org

For industry information, contact
Air-Conditioning, Heating, and Refrigeration Institute
4100 North Fairfax Drive, Suite 200
Arlington, VA 22203-1678

Tel: 703-524-8800
Email: ahri@ahrinet.org
http://www.ahrinet.org

For information on careers, contact
American Society of Heating, Refrigerating and Air-Conditioning Engineers
1791 Tullie Circle, NE
Atlanta, GA 30329-2305
Tel: 800-527-4723
Email: ashrae@ashrae.org
http://www.ashrae.org

Check out the following Web site, created by a coalition of organizations representing the heating, air-conditioning, and refrigeration industry:
Cool Careers
http://www.coolcareers.org

For information on state apprenticeship programs, visit
Employment & Training Administration
U.S. Department of Labor
http://www.doleta.gov

For information on accredited programs and certification, contact
HVAC Excellence
PO Box 491
Mt. Prospect, IL 60056-0521
Tel: 800-394-5268
http://www.hvacexcellence.org

For information on certification programs, contact
North American Technician Excellence
2111 Wilson Boulevard, #510
Arlington, VA 22201-3051
http://www.natex.org

For information on accredited training programs, contact
Partnership for Air-Conditioning, Heating, Refrigeration Accreditation
4100 North Fairfax Drive, Suite 210
Arlington, VA 22203-1623
http://www.pahrahvacr.org

For information on union membership, contact
Plumbing-Heating-Cooling Contractors Association
PO Box 6808
180 South Washington Street
Falls Church, VA 22046-2900
Tel: 800-533-7694
Email: naphcc@naphcc.org
http://www.phccweb.org

For information on industrial plant refrigeration certification, contact
Refrigerating Engineers & Technicians Association
PO Box 1819
Salinas, CA 93902-1819
Tel: 831-455-8783
Email: info@reta.com
http://www.reta.com

Landscape Architects

OVERVIEW

Landscape architects plan and design areas such as highways, housing communities, college campuses, commercial centers, recreation facilities, and nature conservation areas. They work to balance beauty and function in developed outdoor areas. There are approximately 26,000 landscape architects employed in the United States.

HISTORY

In the United States landscape architecture has been a profession for the last 100 years. During the early part of the 20th century, landscape architects worked mainly for the wealthy or the government on public-works projects. In 1918 the practice of dividing large plots of land into individual lots for sale was born. In addition, there was a new public interest in the development of outdoor recreational facilities. These two factors provided many new opportunities for landscape architects.

The most dramatic growth occurred following the environmental movement of the 1960s, when public respect for protection of valuable natural resources reached an all-time high. Landscape architects have played a key role in encouraging the protection of natural resources while providing for the increasing housing and recreation needs of the American public.

In the last 30 years, the development of recreational areas has become more important as has the development of streets, bypasses, and massive highways. Landscape architects are needed in most projects of this nature. Both developers and community planners draw upon the services of landscape architects now more than ever.

THE JOB

Landscape architects plan and design outdoor spaces that make the best use of the land and at the same time respect the needs of the natural environment. They may be involved in a number of different types of projects, including the design of parks or gardens, scenic roads, housing projects, college or high school campuses, country clubs, cemeteries, or golf courses. They work in both the public and private sectors.

Landscape architects begin a project by carefully reviewing their client's desires, including the purpose, structures needed, and funds available. They study the work site itself, observing and mapping such features as the slope of the land, existing structures, plants, and trees. They also consider different views of the location, taking note of shady and sunny areas, the structure of the soil, and existing utilities.

Landscape architects consult with a number of different people, such as engineers, architects, city officials, zoning experts, real estate agents and brokers, and landscape nursery workers to develop a complete understanding of the job. Then they develop detailed plans and drawings of the site to present to the client for approval. Some projects take many months before the proposed plans are ready to be presented to the client.

After developing final plans and drawing up a materials list, landscape architects invite construction companies to submit bids for the job. Depending upon the nature of the project and the contractual agreement, landscape architects may remain on the job to supervise construction, or they may leave the project once work has begun. Those who remain on the job serve as the client's representative until the job is completed and approved.

REQUIREMENTS

High School

To prepare for a college program in landscape architecture, take courses in English composition and literature; social sciences, including history, government, and sociology; natural sciences, including biology, chemistry, and physics; and mathematics. If available, take drafting and mechanical drawing courses to begin building the technical skills needed for the career.

Postsecondary Training

A bachelor's or master's degree in landscape architecture is usually the minimum requirement for entry into this field. Undergraduate and graduate programs in landscape architecture are offered in various colleges and universities; 79 programs at 67 colleges and universities are accredited by the Landscape Architectural Accreditation Board of the American Society of Landscape Architects (ASLA). Courses of study usually focus on six basic areas of the profession: landscape design, landscape construction, plants, architecture, graphic expression (mechanical, freehand, and computer-based drawings), and verbal expression.

Hands-on work is a crucial element to the curriculum. Whenever possible, students work on real projects to gain experience with computer-aided design programs and video simulation.

Certification or Licensing
Almost all states require landscape architects to be licensed. To obtain licensure, applicants must pass the Landscape Architect Registration Examination, sponsored by the Council of Landscape Architectural Registration Boards (CLARB). Though standards vary by state, most require applicants to have a degree from an accredited program and to be working toward one to four years of experience in the field. In addition, 13 states require prospective landscape architects to pass another exam that tests knowledge of local environmental regulations, vegetation, and other characteristics unique to the particular state. Because these standards vary, landscape architects may have to reapply for licensure if they plan to work in a different state. However, in many cases, workers who meet the national standards and have passed the exam may be granted the right to work elsewhere. For more information on licensing, contact CLARB (http://www.clarb.org) or ASLA (http://www.asla.org).

Landscape architects working for the federal government need a bachelor's or master's degree but do not need to be licensed.

Other Requirements
You should be interested in art and nature and have good business sense, especially if you hope to work independently. Interest in environmental protection, community improvement, and landscape design is also crucial for the profession. You should also be flexible and be able to think creatively to solve unexpected problems that may develop during the course of a project.

EXPLORING

If you are interested in learning more about the field, you can gather information and experience in a number of ways. Apply for

Read More About It

Allen, Edward, and Joseph Iano. *Fundamentals of Building Construction: Materials and Methods.* 5th ed. Hoboken, N.J.: Wiley, 2008.

Gisler, Margaret. *Careers for Hard Hats and Other Construction Types.* 2d ed. New York: McGraw-Hill, 2008.

Pasternak, Ceel. *Cool Careers for Girls in Construction.* Manassas Park, Va.: Impact Publications, 2000.

Sumichrast, Michael. *Opportunities in Building Construction Careers.* New York: McGraw-Hill, 2007.

a summer internship with a landscape architectural firm or at least arrange to talk with someone in the job. Ask them questions about their daily duties, the job's advantages and disadvantages, and if they recommend any landscape architecture programs. Finally, you can take the Landscape Architecture Interest Test at the ASLA Web site (http://www.asla.org) to gauge your interest in the field.

EMPLOYERS

There are approximately 26,700 landscape architects employed in the United States. More than 50 percent of landscape architects are employed in architectural, engineering, and related services. Landscape architects work in every state in the United States, in small towns and cities as well as heavily populated areas. Some work in rural areas, such as those who plan and design parks and recreational areas. However the majority of positions are found in suburban and urban areas.

Landscape architects work for a variety of different employers in both the public and private sectors. They may work with a school board planning a new elementary or high school, with manufacturers developing a new factory, with homeowners improving the land surrounding their home, or with a city council planning a new suburban development.

In the private sector, most landscape architects do some residential work, though few limit themselves entirely to projects with individual homeowners. Larger commercial or community projects are usually more profitable. Workers in the public sector plan and design government buildings, parks, and public lands. They also may conduct studies on environmental issues and restore lands such as mines or landfills.

STARTING OUT

After graduating from a landscape architecture program, you can usually receive job assistance from the school's career services office. Although these services do not guarantee a job, they can be helpful in making initial contacts. Many positions are posted by ASLA and published in its two journals, *Landscape Architecture News Digest Online* (http://land.asla.org) and *Landscape Architecture* (http://archives.asla.org/nonmembers/lam.html). Government positions are normally filled through civil service examinations. Information regarding vacancies may be obtained through the local, state, or federal civil service commissions.

Most new hires are often referred to as interns or apprentices until they have gained initial experience in the field and have passed the necessary examinations. Apprentices' duties vary by employer; some handle background project research, others are directly involved in planning and design. Whatever their involvement, all new hires work under the direct supervision of a licensed landscape architect. All drawings and plans must be signed and sealed by the licensed supervisor for legal purposes.

ADVANCEMENT

After obtaining licensure and gaining work experience in all phases of a project's development, landscape architects can become project managers, responsible for overseeing the entire project and meeting schedule deadlines and budgets. They can also advance to the level of associate, increasing their earning opportunities by gaining a profitable stake in a firm.

The ultimate objective of many landscape architects is to gain the experience necessary to organize and open their own firm. According to the U.S. Department of Labor, approximately 21 percent of all landscape architects are self-employed—approximately two times the average of workers in other professions. After the initial investment in computer-aided design software, few start-up costs are involved in breaking into the business independently.

EARNINGS

Salaries for landscape architects vary depending on the employer, work experience, location, and whether they are paid a straight salary or earn a percentage of a firm's profits.

According to 2008 data from the U.S. Department of Labor, the median annual salary for landscape architects was $58,960. The lowest paid 10 percent earned less than $36,520 and the highest paid 10 percent earned more than $97,370. The average salary for those working for the federal government in 2008 was $80,830.

Benefits also vary depending on the employer but usually include health insurance coverage, paid vacation time, and sick leave. Many landscape architects work for small landscaping firms or are self-employed. These workers generally receive fewer benefits than those who work for large organizations.

WORK ENVIRONMENT

Landscape architects spend much of their time in the field gathering information at the work site. They also spend time in the office, drafting plans and designs. Those working for larger organizations may have to travel further away to work sites.

Work hours are generally regular, except during periods of increased business or when nearing a project deadline. Hours vary for self-employed workers because they determine their own schedules.

OUTLOOK

According to the *Occupational Outlook Handbook,* the employment of landscape architects is expected to increase much faster than the average for all occupations through 2018. The increase in demand for landscape architects is a result of several factors: growth of the construction industry, the availability of government funding for surface transportation and transit programs (such as interstate highway construction and maintenance, and pedestrian and bicycle trails), the need to refurbish existing sites, and the increase in city and environmental planning and historic preservation. In addition, many job openings are expected to result from the need to replace experienced workers who leave the field. The U.S. Department of Labor predicts that, in the future, landscape architects will be needed to help "manage stormwater run-off to avoid pollution of waterways and conserve water resources . . . and preserve and restore wetlands and other environmentally sensitive sites."

The need for landscape architecture depends to a great extent on the construction industry. In the event of an economic downturn, when real estate transactions and the construction business is expected to drop off, opportunities for landscape architects will also dwindle.

Opportunities will be the greatest for workers who develop strong technical skills. The growing use of technology such as computer-aided design (CAD) will not diminish the demand for landscape architects. New and improved techniques will be used to create better designs more efficiently rather than reduce the number of workers needed to do the job.

FOR MORE INFORMATION

For information on the career, accredited education programs, licensure requirements, and available publications, contact
American Society of Landscape Architects
636 Eye Street, NW
Washington, DC 20001-3736
Tel: 202-898-2444
http://www.asla.org

For information on student resources, license examinations, and continuing education, contact
Council of Landscape Architectural Registration Boards
3949 Pender Drive, Suite 120
Fairfax, VA 22030-6088
Tel: 571-432-0332
Email: Info@Clarb.org
http://www.clarb.org

For career and educational information, visit the following Web site sponsored by the Landscape Architecture Foundation:
Landscape Architecture
http://www.laprofession.org

Marble Setters, Tile Setters, and Terrazzo Workers

OVERVIEW

Marble setters, tile setters, and *terrazzo workers* are employed in the masonry and stonework trades covering interior and exterior walls, floors, and other surfaces with marble, tile, and terrazzo. Setters in each of these distinct trades work primarily with the material indicated by their title.

These workers are employed in the general construction industries building such things as libraries, schools, hospitals, and apartment complexes. Terrazzo workers tend to be most concentrated in the warm states of Texas, California, and Florida. There are approximately 76,000 tile and marble setters employed in the United States.

HISTORY

Marble is a limestone that is quarried and mined in many countries. The temples of Greece and the ruins of Rome are testimony that marble setters have been using this type of stone as a building material for thousands of years. Statuary marble, the purest form of marble, is white with a crystalline structure. Skilled tradesmen of ancient Greece used it to build such structures as the Propylae (the gateway to the Acropolis) and the Parthenon. Many of Michelangelo's works are made of this marble, and sculptors today continue to use it. However, products such as steel and concrete have generally replaced marble as a building material,

QUICK FACTS

School Subjects
Art
Technical/shop

Personal Skills
Artistic
Mechanical/manipulative

Work Environment
Primarily indoors
Primarily multiple locations

Minimum Education Level
High school diploma
Apprenticeship

Salary Range
$22,140 to $39,210 to
$67,390+

Certification or Licensing
None available

Outlook
Faster than the average

DOT
861

GOE
06.02.01

NOC
7283, 9414

O*NET-SOC
47-2022.00, 47-2044.00,
47-2051.00, 47-2053.00

though it continues to be used on interiors and to some extent on the exteriors of commercial, government, and institutional buildings.

In ancient Greece and Rome, tile setters used marble, clay, and bronze tiles for making roofs. In medieval China, yellow glazed roof tiles with heavy design were used for temples; unglazed roof tiles were often black, suggesting a different firing method from that used for European tiles. Modern architects sometimes still employ large cast-cement roof tiles.

In the 1500s Venetians developed terrazzo (small pieces of broken stone set in mortar and polished in place) and began using it as a building material. Today's terrazzo workers use this very decorative technique mainly for flooring.

THE JOB

Part builders and part artists, marble setters, tile setters, and terrazzo workers work on newly constructed or remodeled buildings. Tile and terrazzo are used mainly on interior building surfaces, while marble (in large pieces) is used primarily as exterior facing.

In marble work, the material to be used is generally delivered to the site ready to be applied, so little cutting and polishing is required. *Machine hoists* and *marble helpers* aid in lifting and carrying large marble blocks. Helpers do most of the mixing of cement and mortar, which leaves the setters free to concentrate on their work. It takes only one look at a wall that has been improperly laid (where the joint lines do not run true) to realize the importance of accuracy for these workers. Where color is used, the appearance of a whole job can be ruined by an improper blending of hues.

When setting marble, the workers first lay out the job. Then they apply a special plaster mixture to the backing material and set the marble pieces in place. These pieces may have to be braced until they are firmly set. Special grout is packed into the joints between the marble pieces, and the joints are slightly indented. This indenting is known as "pointing up."

Tile setters attach tile (thin slabs of clay or stone) to floors, walls, and ceilings with mortar or specially prepared tile cement. They set a sheet of metal mesh to the surface to be tiled and then apply the cement to it, raking it with a tool similar to a yard rake. When this "scratch coat" has dried, setters put a second coat of cement to the mesh and to the tiles and set the tiles in place. Some smaller-sized tile comes in sheets made by fastening a number of tiles to a special paper backing so that they do not have to be set individually. Glassy, non-porous tile is used primarily for floors, and duller, more porous tile is used for walls. After the tile is set in place, the setters tap it with a block of wood or a tool handle to even out the surface. They finish by applying grout (a fine cement) to the set tile, scraping it with a tool to remove the excess grout and wiping it with a wet sponge.

Terrazzo workers lay a base (first course) of fine, dry concrete and level it with a straightedge. They then place metal strips wherever a joint will be placed or where design or color delineations are to be made. This metal stripping is embedded in the first course of concrete. Then the terrazzo workers pour the top course of concrete—a mortar containing marble or granite chips—and roll and level it. Different-colored stone chips are used to color whatever pattern has been planned for the finished floor. In a few days, after the concrete has hardened, the floor is ground smooth and polished with large polishing machines.

Unlike many construction jobs, these occupations are relatively free from routine. Each job is slightly different, and workers rely on their training and ingenuity to a great extent. Marble setters, tile setters, and terrazzo workers generally do not have immediate supervisors on the job. They often manage their own time, schedule and plan their work, and have the responsibility of doing whatever is necessary to provide the best possible job. Seeing an entire project to completion, from start to finish, is a unique and satisfying aspect of this work.

REQUIREMENTS

High School

If you want to apply for jobs in these three trades, you should be at least 17 or 18 years old to qualify for labor-management apprenticeship programs. You should also have graduated from high school or have received a GED. Take at least some courses that involve using hand tools, reading blueprints, and taking precise measurements. Other courses that will be helpful include general math and core English. Taking art courses will increase your knowledge and perception of colors (which is helpful in the marble and tile trades), and many vocational courses will help you improve your manual dexterity. In addition, since being in good physical condition is often necessary in these jobs, participate in sports and general physical education classes.

Postsecondary Training

The best way to train for work in these masonry and tile trades is to participate in an apprenticeship program. In each of these trades, such programs are sponsored by local unions, professional associations such as the International Masonry Institute, and contractors.

Women in Construction

Only 10 percent of workers in the construction industry are women despite the fact that women make up approximately 51 percent of the U.S. population. Although the percentage of women pursuing careers in construction is growing, they still face many challenges (such as sexual harassment and unequal pay) when entering the field. The following organizations provide support to women in the construction industry:

National Association of Women in Construction
http://www.nawic.org

Nontraditional Employment for Women
http://www.new-nyc.org

Tradeswomen Inc.
http://tradeswomen.org

Tradeswomen Now and Tomorrow
http://www.tradeswomennow.org

Women Construction Owners and Executives, USA
http://www.wcoeusa.org

Women Contractors Association
http://www.womencontractors.org

Apprenticeships usually consist of about three years of on-the-job training and related classroom instruction. In on-the-job training, you learn from professional setters how to handle the tools and other materials of the job. You'll get used to such jobs as edging, jointing, and using a straightedge. In class, you will learn blueprint reading, layout work, basic mathematics, safety, cost estimating, and shop practice.

Other Requirements

As with other jobs in the building industries, it is often necessary to have a driver's license so you can operate vehicles on the job and get to job sites that are not accessible by public transportation. You may be required to pass a physical exam and written test at the end of your apprenticeship. You should enjoy demanding work and be disciplined and motivated enough to do your job without close and constant supervision. The ability to get along with coworkers is important, as many employees in these trades work in teams.

EXPLORING

Find an interesting construction site and watch workers and apprentices on their jobs. Find out about the International Masonry Institute's National Training Center in Bowie, Maryland. Once you become an apprentice, you could try to qualify for its program, which includes housing, food, and a nominal wage.

During one of your summer vacations, try to get some work at construction sites or for general contractors; the work may include mixing mortar, carrying, lifting, and keeping the work area clean.

Finally, if you have access to the Internet, one of the easiest ways to explore these trades is to check out the Web sites of such organizations as the International Masonry Institute (http://www.imiweb. org) and the International Union of Bricklayers and Allied Craftworkers (http://www.bacweb.org). These sites will provide information on training and apprenticeship programs.

EMPLOYERS

Approximately 76,000 tile and marble setters are employed in the United States. Marble, tile, and terrazzo workers are employed mainly in the construction industries in cities and towns. Most of those who work with terrazzo have jobs with specialty contractors installing artistic, decorative floors and walls; some are self-employed and may specialize in small jobs. Tile setters are more often self-employed, working on smaller, residential projects like bathrooms and kitchens.

STARTING OUT

If you are interested in this work, you should explore apprenticeship programs. In addition, the local office of your state employment service may be a source of information about apprenticeship training and other programs. Local offices of workers' unions can help, as well as local contractors, who often advertise job openings in the help wanted ads.

Although formal three-year apprenticeships are often available in these trades, many workers learn the work informally by working a certain number of years as a helper, watching and participating in the work firsthand with experienced craftspeople.

After being accepted for a job, new employees are referred for clearance to the union and, after a period of time working, are given positions as helpers. When an opening occurs for a skilled worker, the best qualified person with the most seniority is recommended for the position.

ADVANCEMENT

Skilled tile, terrazzo, and marble setters may become supervisors with the responsibility of managing work crews for large contractors. They can also become self-employed and do contracting on their own. Self-employed contractors must know not only the skills of the trade but also the principles of business. These skills include sales, bidding, bookkeeping, and supervising workers.

EARNINGS

According to the U.S. Department of Labor, median hourly earnings of tile and marble setters were $18.85 in 2008. The middle 50 percent earned between $13.71 and $25.19. Wages ranged from less than $10.65 to more than $32.40 an hour. Earnings of tile and marble setters vary greatly by geographic location and by union membership. The highest wages are paid in urban areas. Earnings for tile setters are usually highest in the North and on the West Coast and lowest in the South.

Terrazo workers earned hourly salaries that ranged from less than $10.82 to $30.12 or more in 2008, according to the U.S. Department of Labor.

Apprentices start at about 50 percent of the skilled worker's salary and increase periodically up to 95 percent during the final stage of the training. Many opportunities are available for overtime work, which usually pays time-and-a-half, or one-and-a-half times the regular wage. Most workers are union members and are thus eligible for the following benefits: retirement plans, hospital and life insurance, and paid holidays and vacations.

WORK ENVIRONMENT

At building sites, tile setters work mostly inside, while marble and terrazzo workers work both indoors and outdoors. Construction sites are often noisy, with different kinds of building equipment being operated. The work is often demanding and requires some strength and physical fitness; workers will find themselves bending, kneeling, lifting, carrying, and reaching. Once they have been given instructions on the details of a particular job, they are expected to work without constant supervision and sometimes with the cooperation of other workers. Most workers can expect 40-hour workweeks when the construction project is proceeding as planned; however, when such elements as inappropriate weather restrict operations, workers may be expected to work fewer hours until conditions change and then overtime when the work continues.

OUTLOOK

Employment for terrazzo workers might increase over the next several years because of the popularity of terrazzo in states like California, Texas, and Florida. Employment for tile and marble setters is expected to grow faster than the average for all careers through 2018, according to the U.S. Department of Labor. Growth will result from more construction of shopping malls, hospitals, schools, restaurants, and other structures in which tile is used extensively, as well as in more expensive homes.

Marble setters, tile setters, and terrazzo workers will find better employment opportunities in more populated urban and suburban areas where more buildings are being constructed and remodeled. Workers may find that work is steadier in climates that allow year-round construction.

FOR MORE INFORMATION

For information on state apprenticeship programs, visit
Employment & Training Administration
U.S. Department of Labor
http://www.doleta.gov

For information on its annual masonry camp for chosen apprentices, contact
International Masonry Institute
The James Brice House
42 East Street
Annapolis, MD 21401-1731
Tel: 410-280-1305
http://www.imiweb.org

For information on training and employment, contact
International Union of Bricklayers and Allied Craftworkers
620 F Street, NW
Washington, DC 20004-1618

Tel: 888-880-8222
Email: askbac@bacweb.org
http://www.bacweb.org

*For information on national standards and continuing educational
seminars, contact*
National Terrazzo & Mosaic Association
201 North Maple Avenue, Suite 208
Purcellville, VA 20132-6102
Tel: 800-323-9736
Email: info@ntma.com
http://www.ntma.com

For information on apprenticeship and training programs, contact
**Operative Plasterers' and Cement Masons' International
   Association**
11720 Beltsville Drive, Suite 700
Beltsville, MD 20705-3104
Tel: 301-623-1000
Email: opcmiaintl@opcmia.org
http://www.opcmia.org

Operating Engineers

OVERVIEW

Operating engineers operate various types of power-driven construction machines, such as shovels, cranes, tractors, bulldozers, pile drivers, concrete mixers, and pumps. There are approximately 404,500 operating engineers employed in the United States.

HISTORY

Although no one knows precisely how they did it, the ancient Egyptians used some type of hoisting system to move the giant stone blocks of the pyramids into place. The Romans constructed roads, viaducts, and bridges of high quality, many of which are still in use today. The Great Wall of China, begun in the 3rd century B.C., remains an amazing architectural feat.

These ancient marvels are even more amazing when one considers that they were all built using only human muscle and simple machines such as levers and pulleys. It was not until the industrial revolution and the invention of the steam engine that complex machines were extensively used in construction. After the harnessing of steam power, Western Europe and America made rapid progress in constructing buildings, roads, and water and sewage systems.

Construction has always played an important role in history. Today, many people measure progress by the increase in new construction in a town or city. All sizes and shapes of construction machinery have been introduced in recent years, and operating engineers work hard to stay current in their training and abilities.

QUICK FACTS

School Subjects
Mathematics
Technical/shop

Personal Skills
Following instructions
Mechanical/manipulative

Work Environment
Primarily outdoors
Primarily multiple locations

Minimum Education Level
Some postsecondary training

Salary Range
$25,930 to $39,270 to $69,340+

Certification or Licensing
None available

Outlook
About as fast as the average

DOT
859

GOE
06.02.03

NOC
7421

O*NET-SOC
47-2073.00, 47-2073.01, 47-2073.02

THE JOB

Operating engineers work for a variety of construction companies as well as manufacturers and state agencies. Whatever the employer, operating engineers run power shovels, cranes, derricks, hoists, pile drivers, concrete mixers, paving machines, trench excavators, bulldozers, tractors, and pumps. They use these machines to move construction materials, earth, logs, coal, grain, and other material. Generally, operating engineers move the materials over short distances: around a construction site, factory, or warehouse or on and off trucks and ships. They also do minor repairs on the equipment, as well as keep them fueled and lubricated. They often are identified by the machines they operate.

Bulldozer operators operate the familiar bulldozer, a tractor-like vehicle with a large blade across the front for moving rocks, trees, earth, and other obstacles from construction sites. They also operate trench excavators, road graders, and similar equipment.

Crane and tower operators lift and move materials, machinery, or other heavy objects with mechanical booms and tower and cable equipment. Although some cranes are used on construction sites, most are used in manufacturing and other industries.

Excavation and loading machine operators handle machinery equipped with scoops, shovels, or buckets to excavate earth at construction sites and to load and move loose materials, mainly in the construction and mining industries.

Hoist and winch operators lift and pull heavy loads using power-operated equipment. Most work in loading operations in construction, manufacturing, logging, transportation, public utilities, and mining.

Operating engineers use various pedals, levers, and switches to run their machinery. For example, crane operators may rotate a crane on its chassis, lift and lower its boom, or lift and lower the load. They also use various attachments for the boom such as buckets, pile drivers, or heavy wrecking balls. When a tall building is being constructed, the crane and its operator may be positioned several hundred feet off the ground.

Operating engineers must have very precise knowledge about the capabilities and limitations of the machines they operate. To avoid tipping over their cranes or damaging their loads, crane operators must be able to judge distance and height and estimate their load size. They must be able to raise and lower the loads with great accuracy. Sometimes operators cannot see the point where the

Operating engineers must have excellent mechanical aptitude and good eye-hand-foot coordination. (*Construction Photography/Corbis*)

load is to be picked up or delivered. At these times, they follow the directions of other workers using hand or flag signals or radio transmissions.

The range of skills of the operating engineer is broader than in most building trades as the machines themselves differ in the ways they operate and the jobs they do. Some operators know how to work several types of machines, while others specialize with one machine.

REQUIREMENTS

High School
A high school education or its equivalent is valuable for the operating engineer and is a requirement for apprenticeship training. Mathematics, physics, and shop classes can provide useful preparation for operating construction equipment.

Postsecondary Training
There are two ways to become an operating engineer: through a union apprentice program or on-the-job training. The apprenticeship, which lasts three years, has at least two advantages: the instruction is more complete, which results in greater employment opportunities, and both labor and management know that the apprentice is training to be a machine operator. Applicants to an apprenticeship program generally must be between the ages of 18 and 30.

Besides learning on the job, the apprentice also receives some classroom instruction in grade-plans reading, elements of electricity, physics, welding, and lubrication services. Despite the advantages of apprenticeships, most apprenticeship programs are difficult to enter because the number of apprentices is limited to the number of skilled workers already in the field.

Other Requirements
Operating engineers must have excellent mechanical aptitude and skillful coordination of eye, hand, and foot movements. In addition, because reckless use of the machinery may be dangerous to other workers, it is necessary to have a good sense of responsibility and seriousness on the job.

Operating engineers should be healthy and strong. They need the temperament to withstand dirt and noise and endure all kinds of weather conditions. Many operating engineers belong to the International Union of Operating Engineers.

EXPLORING

You may be able to gain practical experience with operating machines by observing them in action during a summer job as a laborer or machine operator's helper. Such jobs may be available on local, state, and federal highway and building construction programs.

EMPLOYERS

Construction equipment operators hold approximately 404,500 jobs in the United States. They work for contractors who build highways, dams, airports, skyscrapers, buildings, and other large-scale projects. They also work for utility companies, manufacturers, factories, mines, steel mills, and other firms that do their own construction work. Many work for state and local public works and highway departments.

STARTING OUT

Once apprentices complete their training, their names are put on a list; as positions open up, they are filled in order from the list of available workers. People who do not complete an apprenticeship program may apply directly to manufacturers, utilities, or contractors who employ operating engineers for entry-level jobs as machine operator's helpers.

ADVANCEMENT

Some operating engineers (generally those with above-average ability and interest, as well as good working habits) advance to job supervisor and occasionally construction supervisor. Some are able to qualify for higher pay by training themselves to operate more complicated machines.

EARNINGS

The median annual salary for all operating engineers and other construction equipment operators was approximately $39,270 in 2008, according to the U.S. Department of Labor. Salaries ranged from less than $25,930 to $69,340 or more a year.

Often, workers are paid by the hour. Rates vary according to the area of the country and the employer. In highway and street construction the mean hourly wage was $23.00 in 2008. Those working in nonresidential building construction earned $23.60 an hour. In local government, operating engineers made approximately $18.29 an hour.

Benefits for operating engineers depend on the employer; however, they usually include such items as health insurance, retirement or 401(k) plans, and paid vacation days.

WORK ENVIRONMENT

Operating engineers consider dirt and noise a part of their jobs. Some of the machines on which they work constantly shake and jolt them. This constant movement, along with the strenuous, outdoor nature of the work, makes this a physically tiring job. Since the work is done almost entirely outdoors in almost any kind of weather, operating engineers must be willing to work under conditions that are often unpleasant.

OUTLOOK

Employment of all operating engineers is projected to grow about as fast as the average for all careers through 2018, according to the U.S. Department of Labor. This is due to an expected increase in residential and nonresidential construction and highway, bridge, and street construction.

However, the construction industry is very sensitive to changes in the overall economy, so the number of openings may fluctuate from year to year. Increased efficiency brought about by automation will also moderate growth to some degree.

FOR MORE INFORMATION

For additional information, contact the following organizations:
Associated General Contractors of America
2300 Wilson Boulevard, Suite 400
Arlington, VA 22201-5426
Tel: 703-548-3118
Email: info@agc.org
http://www.agc.org

International Union of Operating Engineers
1125 17th Street, NW
Washington, DC 20036-4701
Tel: 202-429-9100
http://www.iuoe.org

Painters and Paperhangers

QUICK FACTS

School Subjects
Mathematics
Technical/shop

Personal Skills
Artistic
Following instructions

Work Environment
Indoors and outdoors
Primarily multiple locations

Minimum Education Level
Apprenticeship

Salary Range
$22,360 to $32,960 to
$69,630

Certification or Licensing
Voluntary

Outlook
About as fast as the average

DOT
840

GOE
06.02.02

NOC
7294

O*NET-SOC
47-2141.00, 47-2142.00,
51-9122.00, 51-9123.00

OVERVIEW

For both practical purposes and aesthetic appeal, building surfaces are often painted and decorated with various types of coverings. Although painting and paperhanging are two separate skills, many building-trades craftsworkers do both types of work. *Painters* apply paints, varnishes, enamels, and other types of finishes to decorate and protect interior and exterior surfaces of buildings and other structures. *Paperhangers* cover interior walls and ceilings with decorative paper, fabric, vinyls, and other types of materials. There are approximately 450,100 painters and paperhangers working in the United States.

HISTORY

The history of the skilled house painter's occupation in this country begins in the 18th century, when American colonists made their own paints for their homes. There were few people in the business of manufacturing paint in the colonies, and it was unusual to order materials from other countries because the shipping and transport industries were not as sophisticated as they are today.

Instead, builders and owners depended on local products for making paint. Milk, for example, was often used as a base. Soil from land that had traces of iron was burned to make paint with a red pigment, or colored tint. Material called lampblack, which is black soot, was also used to make pigmented paint. In 1867 manufacturers made available the first prepared paints. After this, machines were invented to enable manufacturers to produce paint in large amounts.

Paperhanging as an occupation probably began around the 16th century. Although the Chinese invented decorative paper, it was the Europeans who first used it to cover walls. Wealthy homeowners often decorated the walls of their rooms with tapestries and velvet hangings (which was often done for warmth as well as decoration); those who could not afford such luxuries would imitate the rich by hanging inexpensive, yet decorative, wallpaper in their homes.

Paperhangers and painters were in great demand as building construction developed on a large scale in the early part of the 20th century. Since the middle of the 20th century, there have been great advancements in the materials and techniques used by these skilled trades workers.

THE JOB

Workers in the painting and paperhanging trades often perform both functions; painters may take on jobs that involve hanging wallpaper, and paperhangers may work in situations where they are responsible for painting walls and ceilings. However, although there is some overlap in the work, each trade has its own characteristic skills.

Painters must be able to apply paint thoroughly, uniformly, and rapidly to any type of surface. To do this, they must be skilled in handling brushes and other painting tools and have a working knowledge of the various characteristics of paints and finishes—their durability, suitability, and ease of handling and application.

Preparation of the area to be painted is an important duty of painters, especially when repainting old surfaces. They first smooth the surface, removing old, loose paint with a scraper, paint remover (usually a liquid solution), wire brush, or paint-removing gun (similar in appearance to a hairdryer) or a combination of these items. If necessary, they remove grease and fill nail holes, cracks, and joints with putty, plaster, or other types of filler. Often, a prime coat or sealer is applied to further smooth the surface and make the finished coat level and well blended in color.

Once the surface is prepared, painters select premixed paints or prepare paint by mixing required portions of pigment, oil, and thinning and drying substances. (For purposes of preparing paint, workers must have a thorough knowledge of the composition of the various materials they use and of which materials mix well together.) They then paint the surface using a brush, spray gun, or roller; choosing the most appropriate tool for applying paint is one of the most important decisions a painter must make because using incorrect tools often slows down the work and produces unacceptable results. Spray guns are used generally for large surfaces or objects that do not lend themselves to brush work, such as lattices, cinder and concrete block, and radiators.

Many painters specialize in working on exterior surfaces only, painting house sidings and outside walls of large buildings. When doing work on tall buildings, scaffolding (raised supportive platforms) must be erected to allow the painter to climb to his or her position at various heights above the ground; workers also might use swinglike and chairlike platforms hung from heavy cables.

The first task of the paperhanger is similar to that of the painter: to prepare the surface to be covered. Rough spots must be smoothed, holes and cracks must be filled, and old paint, varnish, and grease must be removed from the surface. In some cases, old wallpaper must be removed by brushing it with solvent, soaking it down with water, or steaming it with portable steamer equipment. In new work, the paperhangers apply sizing, which is a prepared glazing material used as filler to make the plaster less porous and to ensure that the paper sticks well to the surface.

After erecting any necessary scaffolding, the paperhangers measure the area to be covered and cut the paper to size. They then mix paste and apply it to the back of the paper, which is then placed on the wall or ceiling and smoothed into place with brushes or rollers. In placing the paper on the wall, paperhangers must make sure that they match any design patterns at the adjacent edges of paper strips, cut overlapping ends, and smooth the seams between each strip.

REQUIREMENTS

High School
Although a high school education is not essential, workers should have at least the equivalent, such as a GED. Shop classes can help prepare you for the manual work involved in painting and paperhanging, while art classes will help you develop an eye for color and design. Chemistry classes will be useful in dealing with the paints, solvents, and other chemicals used in this work.

Postsecondary Training

To qualify as a skilled painter or paperhanger, a person must complete either an apprenticeship or an on-the-job training program. The apprenticeship program, which often combines painting and paperhanging, consists of three years of carefully planned activity, including work experience and related classroom instruction (approximately 144 hours of courses each year). During this period, the apprentice becomes familiar with all aspects of the craft: use of tools and equipment, preparation of surfaces as well as of paints and pastes, application methods, coordination of colors, reading blueprints, characteristics of wood and other surfaces, cost-estimating methods, and safety techniques. Courses often involve mathematics and practice sessions on the techniques of the trade.

A painter uses a roller to apply paint to a wall. *(Photo Disc)*

On-the-job training programs involve learning the trade informally while working for two to three years under the guidance of experienced painters or paperhangers. The trainees usually begin as helpers until they acquire the necessary skills and knowledge for more difficult jobs. Workers without formal apprenticeship training are more easily accepted in these crafts than in most of the other building trades.

Certification or Licensing
NACE International offers the protective coating specialist designation to painters who are interested in working in industrial settings. Contact the organization for more information.

Other Requirements
Basic skills requirements are the same for both painters and paperhangers. Most employers prefer to hire applicants who are in good physical condition, with manual dexterity and a good sense of color. For protection of their own health, applicants should not be allergic to paint fumes or other materials used in the trade.

EXPLORING
You can explore the work of painters and paperhangers by reading trade journals and watching instructional videos or television programs. Those who already have some experience in the trade should keep up with the news by reading such publications as the monthly *Painters and Allied Trades Journal*, available to members of the International Union of Painters and Allied Trades union (http://www.iupat.org/about/publications.html). Look for educational books and DVDs at your local library. The projects tackled on television home improvement shows almost always feature the work of painters or paperhangers to some extent.

Certainly, painting and paperhanging in your own home or apartment provide valuable firsthand experience. Also valuable is the experience gained with a part-time or summer job as a helper to skilled workers who are already in the trade. Those who have done satisfactory part-time work sometimes go to work full time for the same employer after a certain period of time.

EMPLOYERS
There are approximately 450,100 painters and paperhangers employed in the United States; most of them are painters and trade

union members. Approximately 42 percent of these workers are self-employed. Jobs are found mainly with contractors who work on projects such as new construction, remodeling, and restoration; others are found as maintenance workers for such establishments as schools, apartment complexes, and high-rise buildings.

STARTING OUT

If you wish to become an apprentice, you should contact employers, your state's employment service bureau or apprenticeship agency, or the union headquarters of the International Union of Painters and Allied Trades. You must, however, have the approval of the joint labor-management apprenticeship committee before you can enter the occupation by this method. If the apprentice program is filled, you may wish to enter the trade as an on-the-job trainee. In this case, you usually should contact employers directly to begin work as a helper.

ADVANCEMENT

Successful completion of one of the two types of training programs is necessary before individuals can become qualified skilled painters or paperhangers. If workers have management ability and good planning skills, and if they work for a large contracting firm, they may advance to the following positions: *supervisor,* who supervises and coordinates activities of other workers; *painting and decorating contract estimator,* who computes material requirements

Earnings for Painters, Construction and Maintenance by Industry, 2008

Field	Mean Annual Earnings
Federal government	$46,210
Local government	$46,010
Nonresidential building construction	$39,610
Building finishing contractors	$35,520
Residential building construction	$33,710

Source: U.S. Department of Labor

and labor costs; or *superintendent,* who oversees a large contract painting job.

Some painters and paperhangers, once they have acquired enough capital and business experience, go into business for themselves as painting and decorating contractors. These self-employed workers must be able to take care of all standard business affairs, such as bookkeeping, insurance and legal matters, advertising, and billing.

EARNINGS

Painters and paperhangers tend to earn more per hour than many other construction workers, but their total annual incomes may be less because of work time lost due to poor weather and periods of layoffs between contract assignments. In 2008 median hourly earnings of painters were $15.85, according to the U.S. Department of Labor. Hourly wages ranged from less than $10.75 to more than $27.16. Paperhangers earned hourly salaries that ranged from less than $10.82 to $33.48 or more. Hourly wage rates for painting and paperhanging apprentices usually start at 40–50 percent of the rate for experienced workers and increase periodically. Wages often vary depending on the geographic location of the job.

Benefits for painters and paperhangers depend on the employer; however, they usually include such items as health insurance, retirement or 401(k) plans, and paid vacation days.

WORK ENVIRONMENT

Most painters and paperhangers work a standard 40-hour week, and they usually earn extra pay for working overtime. Their work requires them to stand for long periods of time, to climb, and to bend. Painters work both indoors and outdoors, because their job may entail painting interior surfaces as well as exterior siding and other areas; paperhangers work exclusively indoors. Because these occupations involve working on ladders and often with electrical equipment such as power sanders and paint sprayers, workers must adhere to safety standards.

OUTLOOK

Employment of painters and paperhangers is expected to grow about as fast as the average for all occupations through 2018, according to the U.S. Department of Labor. Opportunities are expected to be excellent for painters, while employment for paperhangers will decline rapidly as a result of consumers' interest in less-expensive design options. Many job openings will occur as workers retire, transfer, or otherwise leave the occupation.

Increased construction will generate a need for more painters to work on new buildings and industrial structures. However, this will also lead to increased competition among self-employed painters and painting contractors for the better jobs. Newer types of paint have made it easier for inexperienced persons to do their own painting, but this does not affect the employment outlook much because most painters and paperhangers work on industrial and commercial projects and are not dependent on residential work.

FOR MORE INFORMATION

For information on state apprenticeship programs, visit
Employment & Training Administration
U.S. Department of Labor
http://www.doleta.gov

For information on union membership, contact
International Union of Painters and Allied Trades
1750 New York Avenue, NW
Washington, DC 20006-5301
Tel: 202-637-0740
Email: mail@iupat.org
http://www.iupat.org

For information about certification for industrial painters, contact
NACE International
1440 South Creek Drive
Houston, TX 77084-4906
Tel: 800-797-6223
http://www.nace.org

For additional information about becoming a painter or paperhanger, contact the following organizations:
National Association of Home Builders
1201 15th Street, NW
Washington, DC 20005-2842

Tel: 800-368-5242
http://www.nahb.com

Painting and Decorating Contractors of America
11960 Westline Industrial Drive, Suite 201
St. Louis, MO 63146-4020
Tel: 800-332-7322
http://www.pdca.org

Plasterers

OVERVIEW

Plasterers apply coats of plaster to interior walls, ceilings, and partitions of buildings to produce fire-resistant and relatively soundproof surfaces. They also work on exterior building surfaces and do ornamental forming and casting work. Their work is similar to that of *drywall workers,* who use drywall rather than plaster to build interior walls and ceilings. There are approximately 49,000 plasterers employed in the United States.

HISTORY

Plastering is one of the most ancient crafts in the building trades. Before current plasters were invented, primitive people used damp clay, sand, grasses, or reeds. They used their hands, stones, and early tools to smooth the surfaces of the walls of their dwellings. The trade has evolved into a highly skilled type of work through the development and use of many new and improved materials and techniques.

THE JOB

Plasterers work on building interiors and exteriors. They apply plaster directly to masonry, wire, wood, metal, or lath. (Lath is a supportive reinforcement made of wood or metal that is attached to studs to form walls and ceilings.) These surfaces are designed to hold the plaster in position until it dries. After checking the specifications and plans made by the builder, architect, or foreman, plasterers put a border of plaster of the desired thickness on the top and bottom of the wall. After this border has hardened sufficiently, plasterers fill in the remaining portion of the wall with

Two plasterers (*far left*) apply plaster to the walls of a new condominium. (*Dick Blume, Syracuse Newspapers/The Image Works*)

two coats of plaster. They then level and smooth the surface of the wall area with a straightedge tool and darby (a long flat tool used for smoothing). Plasterers then apply the third or finishing coat of plaster, which is the last operation before painting or paperhanging. This coat may be finished to an almost velvet smoothness or into one of a variety of decorative textures used in place of papering.

When plastering cinder block and concrete, plasterers first apply the brown coat—a base of gypsum plaster. The second coat, called the white coat, is lime-based plaster. When plastering metal lath foundations, they first apply a scratch coat with a trowel, spread it over the lath, and scratch the surface with a rake-like tool to make ridges before it dries so that the next coat—the brown coat—will bond tightly. Next, the plasterer sprays or trowels the plaster for the brown coat and smoothes it. The finishing coat is either sprayed on or applied with a hawk and trowel. Plasterers also use brushes and water for the finishing coat. The final coat is a mix of lime, water, and plaster of paris that sets quickly and is smooth and durable.

The plasterer sometimes works with plasterboard or sheetrock, which are types of wallboard that come ready for installation. When working with such wallboard, the plasterer cuts and fits the wallboard to the studding and joists of ceilings and interior walls. When installing ceilings, plasterers work as a team.

Plasterers who specialize in exterior plastering are known as *stucco masons*. They apply a weather-resistant decorative covering of Portland cement plaster to lath in the same manner as interior plastering or with the use of a spray gun. In exterior work, however, the finish coat usually consists of a mixture of white cement and sand or a patented finish material that may be applied in a variety of colors and textures.

Decorative and ornamental plastering is the specialty of highly skilled *molding plasterers*. This work includes molding or forming and installing ornamental plaster panels and trim. Some molding plasterers also cast intricate cornices and recesses used for indirect lighting. Such work is rarely done today because of the great degree of skill involved and the high cost.

In recent years most plasterers have begun using machines to spray plaster on walls, ceilings, and structural sections of buildings. Machines that mix plaster have been in general use for many years.

REQUIREMENTS

High School

Although a high school or trade school education is not mandatory for this career, it is highly recommended. In high school or vocational school, you should take mechanical drawing, drafting, woodwork, and other shop courses. Classes in mathematics will sharpen your skills in the applied mathematics of layout work.

Postsecondary Training

To qualify as a journeyman plasterer, you must complete either an apprenticeship or on-the-job training program. The apprenticeship program consists of three to four years of carefully planned activity combined with approximately 6,000–8,000 hours of work experience and an annual 144 hours of related classroom instruction. An apprenticeship is usually the best start, since it includes on-the-job training as well as formal instruction.

On-the-job training consists of working for four or more years under the supervision of experienced plasterers. The trainee usually begins as a helper or laborer and learns the trade informally by observing or being taught by other plasterers.

Certification or Licensing

Voluntary certification is available from the International Masonry Institute, a subsidiary of the International Union of Bricklayers and Allied Craftworkers. Contact the institute for more information.

Other Requirements

Most employers prefer to hire applicants who are at least 17 years old, in good physical condition, and have a high degree of manual dexterity.

EXPLORING

To observe the plasterer at work, ask your school counselor to arrange a field trip to a construction site or try to arrange one on your own. An excellent firsthand experience in this trade would be to obtain a part-time or summer job as a plasterer's helper or laborer.

EMPLOYERS

Approximately 49,000 plasterers are employed in the United States. Most plasterers work for independent plastering contractors and are members of unions, either the Operative Plasterers' and Cement Masons' International Association or the International Union of Bricklayers and Allied Craftworkers.

STARTING OUT

Those who wish to become apprentices usually contact local plastering contractors, their state's employment service bureau, or the appropriate union headquarters. In most places, the local branch of the Operative Plasterers' and Cement Masons' International Association is the best place to inquire about apprenticeships. The U.S. Department of Labor's Employment and Training Administration (http://www.doleta.gov/OA/eta_de fault.cfm) and your state's employment office are also good places to contact for information.

If the apprenticeship program is filled, applicants may wish to enter the field as on-the-job trainees. In this case, they usually contact a plastering contractor directly and begin work as helpers or laborers. They learn about the work by mixing the plaster, helping plasterers with scaffolding, and carrying equipment.

ADVANCEMENT

Most plasterers learn the full range of plastering skills. They develop expertise in finish plastering as well as rough coat plastering. They also learn the spray gun technique and become proficient spray gun plasterers. With additional training, they may specialize in exterior work as stucco masons or in ornamental plastering as molding plasterers.

If they have certain personal characteristics such as the ability to deal with people and good judgment and planning skills, plasterers may progress to become supervisors or job estimators. Many plasterers become self-employed, and some eventually become contractors.

EARNINGS

The median hourly wage for plasterers was about $18.01 in 2008, according to the U.S. Department of Labor. Wages ranged from less than $12.01 to more than $29.59 an hour. Plasterers in Napa, California; Springfield, Illinois; Boston; Chicago; Tacoma, Washington; and other large cities received the highest hourly earnings. Plasterers may receive traditional fringe benefits, such as health insurance and paid vacation days.

WORK ENVIRONMENT

Most plasterers work 40 hours a week with occasional overtime when necessary to meet a contract deadline. Overtime work is usually compensated at the rate of one and a half times the regular hourly wage. The workday may start earlier than most (7:00 A.M.), but it also usually ends earlier (3:00 P.M.). Some plasterers face layoffs between jobs, while others may work with drywall or ceiling tile as required by their contractors when there is no plastering work to be done.

Most of the work is performed indoors, plastering walls and ceilings and forming and casting ornamental designs. Plasterers also work outdoors, doing stucco work and Exterior Insulated Finish Systems (exterior systems that include Styrofoam insulation board and two thin coats of polymer and acrylic modified materials). They often work with other construction workers, including carpenters, plumbers, and pipefitters. Plasterers must do a considerable amount of standing, stooping, and lifting. They often get plaster on their work clothes and dust in their eyes and noses. Plasterers take pride in seeing the results of their work—something they have helped to build that will last a long time. Their satisfaction with progress on the job, day by day, may be a great deal more than in jobs where the worker never sees the completed product or where the results are less obvious.

As highly skilled workers, plasterers have higher earnings, better chances for promotion, and more opportunity to go into business for themselves than other workers. They also can usually find jobs in almost any part of the United States.

OUTLOOK

Employment opportunities for plasterers are expected to increase about as fast as the average for all careers through 2018, according to the U.S. Department of Labor. Plasterers' employment prospects usually rise and fall with the economy, and especially with the health of the construction industry.

Recent improvements in both plastering materials and methods of application are expected to increase the scope of the craft and create more job opportunities, especially in urban areas of the Northeast. To name a few such developments: more lightweight plasters are being used because of excellent soundproofing, acoustical, and fireproofing qualities; machine plastering, insulating, and fireproofing are becoming more widespread; and the use of plaster veneer or high-density plaster in creating a finished surface is being used increasingly in new buildings. Plaster veneer, or thin-coat plastering, is a thin coat of plaster that can be finished in one coat. It is made of lime and plaster of paris and can be mixed with water at the job site. It is often applied to a special gypsum base on interior surfaces. Exterior systems have also changed to include Styrofoam insulation board and Exterior Insulated Finish Systems.

Opportunities for stucco masons will be best in Florida, California, and the Southwest—areas in which the use of stucco is popular.

FOR MORE INFORMATION

For information on the wall and ceiling industry, contact
Association of the Wall and Ceiling Industries, International
803 West Broad Street, Suite 600
Falls Church, VA 22046-3108
Tel: 703-538-1600
http://www.awci.org

For information on state apprenticeship programs, visit
Employment & Training Administration
U.S. Department of Labor
http://www.doleta.gov

For information on the lath and plaster industry, contact
International Institute for Lath and Plaster
PO Box 1663
Lafayette, CA 94549-1663
http://www.iilp.org

For information on certification, contact
International Masonry Institute
The James Brice House
42 East Street
Annapolis, MD 21401-1731
Tel: 410-280-1305
http://imiweb.org

For information about construction trades, training, and union membership, contact
International Union of Bricklayers and Allied Craftworkers
620 F Street, NW
Washington, DC 20004-1618
Tel: 888-880-8222
Email: askbac@bacweb.org
http://www.bacweb.org

For information on membership and apprenticeships, contact
Operative Plasterers' and Cement Masons' International Association
11720 Beltsville Drive, Suite 700
Beltsville, MD 20705-3104
Tel: 301-623-1000
Email: opcmiaintl@opcmia.org
http://www.opcmia.org

Plumbers and Pipefitters

OVERVIEW

Plumbers and *pipefitters* assemble, install, alter, and repair pipes and pipe systems that carry water, steam, air, or other liquids and gases for sanitation and industrial purposes as well as other uses. Plumbers also install plumbing fixtures, appliances, and heating and refrigerating units. There are approximately 494,700 plumbers and pipefitters working in the United States.

HISTORY

Although the early Egyptians are known to have used lead pipes to carry water and drainage into and out of buildings, the use of plumbing in a citywide system was first achieved in the Roman Empire. In Renaissance times, the techniques of plumbing were revived and used in some of the great castles and monasteries. But, the greatest advances in plumbing were made in the 19th century, when towns grew into cities and the need for adequate public sanitation was recognized.

THE JOB

Because little difference exists between the work of the plumber and the pipefitter in most cases, the two are often considered to be one trade. However, some craftsworkers specialize in one field or the other, especially in large cities.

The work of pipefitters differs from that of plumbers mainly in its location and the variety and size of pipes used. Plumbers work primarily in residential and commercial buildings, whereas pipefitters are generally employed by large industrial concerns—such as oil refineries, refrigeration plants, and defense establishments—where more complex systems of piping are used. Plumbers assemble, install, and repair heating, water, and drainage systems, especially those that must be connected to public utilities systems. Some of their jobs include replacing burst pipes and installing and repairing sinks, bathtubs, water heaters, hot water tanks, garbage disposal units, dishwashers, and water softeners. Plumbers also may work on septic tanks, cesspools, and sewers. During the final construction stages of both commercial and residential buildings, plumbers install heating and air-conditioning units and connect radiators, water heaters, and plumbing fixtures.

Most plumbers follow set procedures in their work. After inspecting the installation site to determine pipe location, they cut and thread pipes, bend them to required angles by hand or machines, and then join them by means of welded, brazed, caulked, soldered, or threaded joints. To test for leaks in the system, they fill the pipes with water or air. Plumbers use a variety of tools, including hand tools such as wrenches, reamers, drills, braces and bits, hammers, chisels, and saws; power machines that cut, bend, and thread pipes; gasoline torches; and welding, soldering, and brazing equipment.

Specialists include diesel engine pipefitters, *steamfitters* (who install pipe systems that facilitate the movement of gases or liquids under high pressure), *sprinklerfitters* (who install automatic fire sprinkler systems), ship and boat building coppersmiths, industrial-gas fitters, gas-main fitters, prefab plumbers, and pipe cutters.

REQUIREMENTS

High School
A high school diploma is especially important for getting into a good apprenticeship program. High school preparation should include courses in mathematics, chemistry, and physics, as well as some shop courses.

Postsecondary Training
To qualify as a plumber, a person must complete either a formal apprenticeship or an informal on-the-job training program. To be considered for the apprenticeship program, individuals must pass an examination administered by their state employment agency and have their qualifications approved by the local joint labor-management apprenticeship committee.

The apprenticeship program for plumbers consists of four or five years of carefully planned activity combining direct training with at least 144 hours of formal classroom instruction each year. The program is designed to give apprentices diversified training by having them work for several different plumbing or pipefitting contractors.

On-the-job training, on the other hand, usually consists of working for five or more years under the guidance of an experienced craftsworker. Trainees begin as helpers until they acquire the necessary skills and knowledge for more difficult jobs. Frequently, they supplement this practical training by taking trade (or correspondence) school courses.

Certification or Licensing
A license is required for plumbers in many places. To obtain this license, plumbers must pass a special examination to demonstrate their knowledge of local building codes as well as their all-around knowledge of the trade. To become a plumbing contractor in most places, a master plumber's license must be obtained.

Other Requirements
To be successful in this field, you should like to solve a variety of problems and should not object to being called on during evenings, weekends, or holidays to perform emergency repairs. As in most service occupations, plumbers should be able to get along well with all kinds of people. You should be a person who works well alone, but who can also direct the work of helpers and enjoy the company of those in the other construction trades.

EXPLORING

Although opportunities for direct experience in this occupation are rare for those in high school, there are ways to explore the field. Speaking to an experienced plumber or pipefitter will give you a clearer picture of day-to-day work in this field. Pursuing hobbies with a mechanical aspect will help you determine how much you like such hands-on work.

EMPLOYERS

Plumbers and pipefitters hold about 494,700 jobs. Approximately 56 percent work for plumbing, heating, and air-conditioning contractors engaged in new construction, repair, modernization, or maintenance work. Approximately 12 percent of plumbers and pipefitters are self-employed.

A plumber replaces a water pipe. *(Jeff Greenberg/The Image Works)*

STARTING OUT

Applicants who wish to become apprentices usually contact local plumbing, heating, and air-conditioning contractors who employ plumbers, the state employment service bureau, or the local branch of the United Association of Journeymen and Apprentices of the Plumbing and Pipe Fitting Industry of the United States and Canada. Individual contractors or contractor associations often sponsor local apprenticeship programs. Apprentices very commonly go on to permanent employment with the firms with which they apprenticed.

ADVANCEMENT

If plumbers have certain qualities, such as the ability to deal with people and good judgment and planning skills, they may progress to such positions as supervisor or job estimator for plumbing or pipefitting contractors. If they work for a large industrial company, they may advance to the position of job superintendent. Many plumbers go into business for themselves. Eventually they may expand their activities and become contractors, employing other workers.

EARNINGS

Plumbers and pipefitters had median earnings of $45,640 in 2008, according to the U.S. Department of Labor. Wages ranged from less than $27,500 to $78,890 or more. Pay rates for apprentices usually start at 50 percent of the experienced worker's rate, and increase by 5 percent every six months until a rate of 95 percent is reached. Benefits for union workers usually include health insurance, sick time, and vacation pay, as well as pension plans.

WORK ENVIRONMENT

Most plumbers have a regular 40-hour workweek with extra pay for overtime. Unlike most of the other building trades, this field is little affected by seasonal factors. The work of the plumber is active and strenuous. Standing for prolonged periods and working in cramped or uncomfortable positions are often necessary. Possible risks include falls from ladders, cuts from sharp tools, and burns from hot pipes or steam. Working with clogged pipes and toilets can also be smelly.

OUTLOOK

Employment opportunities for plumbers (especially those with welding skills) are expected to be very good through 2018, according to the U.S. Department of Labor. This is one of the largest and top-paying careers in the construction industry, and many opportunities will be available. Construction projects are usually only short-term in nature and more plumbers will find steady work in renovation, repair, and maintenance. Since pipework is becoming more important in large industries, more workers will be needed for installation and maintenance work, especially where refrigeration and air-conditioning equipment are used. Pipefitters and steamfitters will enjoy good prospects as a result of the need for continued maintenance and new construction of factories, office buildings, and power plants. Changes in state laws regarding fire protection in businesses and homes should increase employment demand for sprinklerfitters. Employment opportunities fluctuate with local economic conditions, although the plumbing industry is less affected by economic trends than other construction trades.

FOR MORE INFORMATION

For information on state apprenticeship programs, visit
Employment & Training Administration
U.S. Department of Labor
http://www.doleta.gov

For more information about becoming a plumber or pipefitter, contact the following organizations:

Plumbing-Heating-Cooling Contractors Association
180 South Washington Street
PO Box 6808
Falls Church, VA 22046-2900
Tel: 800-533-7694
http://www.phccweb.org

United Association of Journeymen and Apprentices of the Plumbing and Pipe Fitting Industry of the United States and Canada
United Association Building
Three Park Place
Annapolis, MD 21401-3687
Tel: 410-269-2000
http://www.ua.org

Roofers

QUICK FACTS

School Subjects
Mathematics
Technical/shop

Personal Skills
Following instructions
Mechanical/manipulative

Work Environment
Primarily outdoors
Primarily multiple locations

Minimum Education Level
Apprenticeship

Salary range
$22,100 to $33,630 to
$59,190

Certification or Licensing
Required by all states

Outlook
More slowly than the average

DOT
866

GOE
06.02.02

NOC
7291

O*NET-SOC
47-2181.00

OVERVIEW

Roofers install and repair roofs of buildings using a variety of materials and methods, including built-up roofing, single-ply roofing systems, asphalt shingles, tile, and slate. They may also waterproof and damp-proof walls, swimming pools, and other building surfaces. Approximately 148,900 roofers are employed in the United States.

HISTORY

Roofs cover buildings and protect their interiors against snow, rain, wind, temperature extremes, and strong sunlight. The earliest roofs were probably thatched with plant materials such as leaves, branches, or straw. With clay or a similar substance pressed into any open spaces, such a roof can provide good protection from the weather. Roofs constructed on frameworks of thick branches or timbers allowed different roof designs to develop, including the flat and pitched, or sloping, forms that are in use today. When brick and stone began to be used in buildings, people could construct domes and vaults, which are roof forms based on arches.

Throughout most of history, flat roofs have been associated with dry climates, where drainage of water off the roof is seldom a concern. In the 19th century, new roofing and building materials made flat roofs an economical alternative to pitched roofs in somewhat wetter conditions, such as those in much of the United States. Today, flat or very slightly sloped roofs are common on commercial buildings and are also used on some residential buildings. Pitched roofs in various forms have been used for many centuries, largely in climates where drainage is a concern. Most houses have pitched roofs.

All roofs must keep out water. There are two basic types of roof covering that do this: separate shingles, or flat pieces of a waterproof material that are placed so that water cannot get through at the joints; and a continuous layer or sheet membrane of a material that is impermeable to water. Different kinds of roofing materials are appropriate for different kinds of roofs, and each material has its own method of application.

The occupation of roofer has developed along with the various kinds of modern roofing materials. Roofers today must know about how the elements in each roofing system are used, and how water, temperature, and humidity affect the roof. While asphalt shingle roofs on homes may require only relatively simple materials and application procedures, large commercial building roofs can involve complex preparation and layering of materials to produce the necessary protective covering.

THE JOB

Although roofers usually are trained to apply most kinds of roofing, they often specialize in either sheet membrane roofing or prepared roofings such as asphalt shingles, slate, or tile.

One kind of sheet membrane roofing is called built-up roofing. Built-up roofing, used on flat roofs, consists of roofing felt (fabric saturated in bitumen, a tar-like material) laid into hot bitumen. To prepare for putting on a built-up roof, roofers may apply a layer of insulation to the bare roof deck. Then they spread molten bitumen over the roof surface, lay down overlapping layers of roofing felt, and spread more hot bitumen over the felt, sealing the seams and making the roof watertight. They repeat this process several times to build up as many layers as desired. They then give the top a smooth finish or embed gravel in the top for a rough surface.

Single-ply roofing, a relatively new roofing method, uses a waterproof sheet membrane and employs any of several different types of chemical products. Some roofing consists of polymeria-modified bituminous compounds that are rolled out in sheets on the building's insulation. The compound may be remelted on the roof by torch or hot anvil to fuse it to or embed it in hot bitumen in a manner similar to built-up roofing. Other single-ply roofing is made of rubber or plastic materials that can be sealed with contact adhesive cements, solvent welding, hot-air welding, or other methods. Still another type of single-ply roofing consists of spray-in-place polyurethane foam with a polymeric coating. Roofers who apply these roofing systems must be trained in the application methods for each system.

Many manufacturers of these systems require that roofers take special courses and receive certification before they are authorized to use the products.

To apply asphalt shingles, a very common roofing on houses, roofers begin by cutting strips of roofing felt and tacking them down over the entire roof. They nail on horizontal rows of shingles, beginning at the low edge of the roof and working up. Sometimes they must cut shingles to fit around corners, vent pipes, and chimneys. Where two sections of roof meet, they nail or cement flashing, which consists of strips of metal or shingle that make the joints watertight.

Tile and slate shingles, which are more expensive types of residential roofing, are installed slightly differently. First, roofing felt is applied over the wood base. Next, the roofers punch holes in the slate or tile pieces so that nails can be inserted, or they embed the tiles in mortar. Each row of shingles overlaps the preceding row.

Metal roofing is applied by specially trained roofers or by sheet metal workers. One type of metal roof uses metal sections shaped like flat pans, soldered together for weatherproofing and attached by metal clips to the wood below. Another kind of metal roofing, called "standing seam roofing," has raised seams where the sections of sheet metal interlock.

Some roofers waterproof and damp-proof walls, swimming pools, tanks, and structures other than roofs. To prepare surfaces for waterproofing, workers smooth rough surfaces and roughen glazed surfaces. They then brush or spray waterproofing material on the surface. Damp-proofing is done by spraying a coating of tar or asphalt onto interior or exterior surfaces to prevent the penetration of moisture.

Roofers use various hand tools in their work, including hammers, roofing knives, mops, pincers, caulking guns, rollers, welders, chalk lines, and cutters.

REQUIREMENTS

High School

Most employers prefer to hire applicants at least 18 years of age who are in good physical condition and have a good sense of balance. Although a high school education or its equivalent is not required, it is generally preferred. Students can also take courses that familiarize them with some of the skills that are a regular part of roofing work. Beneficial courses include shop, basic mathematics, and mechanical drawing.

Postsecondary Training

Roofers learn the skills they need through on-the-job training or by completing an apprenticeship. Most roofers learn informally on the job while they work under the supervision of experienced roofers. Beginners start as helpers, doing simple tasks like carrying equipment and putting up scaffolding. They gradually gain the skills and knowledge they need for more difficult tasks. Roofers may need four or more years of on-the-job training to become familiar with all the materials and techniques they need to know.

Apprenticeship programs generally provide more thorough, balanced training. Apprenticeships are three years in length and combine a planned program of work experience with formal classroom instruction in related subjects. The work portion of the apprenticeship includes a minimum of 1,400 hours each year under the guidance of experienced roofers. The classroom instruction, at least 144 hours per year, covers such topics as safety practices, how to use and care for tools, and arithmetic.

Certification or Licensing

In addition to apprenticeship experience or on-the-job training, all roofers should receive safety training that is in compliance with standards set by the Occupational Safety and Health Administration (OSHA). Workers can get safety training through their employer or through OSHA's Outreach Training Program.

In addition, the National Roofing Contractors Association provides various educational resources, including seminars, customized training programs, and certificate programs.

Other Requirements

A roofer with a fear of heights will not get far in his or her career. Roofers need a good sense of balance and good hand-eye coordination. Since this work can be dangerous, roofers need to pay attention to detail and be able to follow directions precisely. They should enjoy working outdoors and working with their hands. Roofers may work with architects and other construction workers as well as interact with customers, so they must be able to work as part of a team. To advance in this field, to the position of estimator for example, a roofer should also have strong communication and math skills.

EXPLORING

High school or vocational school students may be able to get first-hand experience of this occupation through a part-time or summer job as a roofer's helper. It may be possible to visit a construction site to observe roofers at work, but a close look is unlikely as roofers do most of their work at heights.

EMPLOYERS

There are approximately 148,900 people employed as roofers in the United States. Most work for established roofing contractors. Approximately 21 percent of roofers are self-employed.

STARTING OUT

People who are planning to start out as helpers and learn on the job can directly contact roofing contractors to inquire about possible openings. Job leads may also be located through the local office of the state employment service or newspaper classified ads. Graduates of vocational schools may get useful information from their schools' career services offices.

People who want to become apprentices can learn about apprenticeships in their area by contacting local roofing contractors, the state employment service, or the local office of the United Union of Roofers, Waterproofers and Allied Workers.

ADVANCEMENT

Experienced roofers who work for roofing contractors may be promoted to supervisory positions in which they coordinate the activities of other roofers. Roofers also may become estimators, calculating the costs of roofing jobs before the work is done. Roofers who have the right combination of personal characteristics, including good judgment, the ability to deal with people, and planning skills, may be able to go into business for themselves as independent roofing contractors.

EARNINGS

The earnings of roofers vary widely depending on how many hours they work, geographical location, skills and experience, and other factors. Sometimes bad weather prevents them from working, and some weeks they work fewer than 20 hours. They make up for lost time in other weeks, and if they work longer hours than the standard workweek (usually 40 hours), they receive extra pay for the overtime. While roofers in northern states may not work in the winter, most roofers work year-round.

In 2008 median hourly earnings of roofers were $16.17, according to the U.S. Department of Labor. Wages ranged from less than $10.63 to more than $28.46.

Hourly rates for apprentices usually start at about 40 to 50 percent of the skilled worker's rate and increase periodically until the pay reaches 90 percent of the full rate during the final six months.

Roofers who work for a company usually receive benefits such as vacation days, sick leave, and health and life insurance. Self-employed or part-time roofers must provide their own benefits.

WORK ENVIRONMENT

Roofers work outdoors most of the time. They work in the heat and cold, but not in wet weather. Roofs can get extremely hot during the summer. The work is physically strenuous, involving lifting heavy weights, prolonged standing, climbing, bending, and squatting. Roofers must work while standing on surfaces that may be steep and quite high; they must use caution to avoid injuries from falls while working on ladders, scaffolding, or roofs.

OUTLOOK

Employment for roofers is expected to increase more slowly than the average for all occupations through 2018, according to the U.S. Department of Labor. However, roofers will continue to be in demand for the construction of new buildings, and roofs tend to need more maintenance and repair work than other parts of buildings. About 75 percent of roofing work is on existing structures. Roofers will always be needed for roof repairs and replacement, even during economic downturns when construction activity generally decreases. Also, damp-proofing and waterproofing are expected to provide an increasing proportion of the work done by roofers.

Turnover in this job is high because roofing work is strenuous, hot, and dirty. Many workers consider roofing a temporary job and move into other construction trades. Since roofing is done during the warmer part of the year, job opportunities will probably be best during spring and summer.

FOR MORE INFORMATION

For information on state apprenticeship programs, visit
Employment & Training Administration
U.S. Department of Labor
http://www.doleta.gov

For information on membership benefits and about becoming a professional roofer, contact

National Roofing Contractors Association
10255 West Higgins Road, Suite 600
Rosemont, IL 60018-5607
Tel: 847-299-9070
http://www.nrca.net

For information on apprenticeships and union membership, contact

United Union of Roofers, Waterproofers and Allied Workers
1660 L Street, NW, Suite 800
Washington, DC 20036-5646
Tel: 202-463-7663
Email: roofers@unionroofers.com
http://www.unionroofers.com

Sheet Metal Workers

OVERVIEW

Sheet metal workers fabricate, assemble, install, repair, and maintain ducts used for ventilating, air-conditioning, and heating systems. They also work with other articles of sheet metal, including roofing, siding, gutters, downspouts, partitions, chutes, and stainless steel kitchen and beverage equipment for restaurants. Not included in this group are employees in factories where sheet metal items are mass-produced on assembly lines. There are approximately 170,700 sheet metal workers employed in the United States.

HISTORY

Sheet metal became important in many products after the development of mills and processes that form various kinds of metal into thin, strong, flat sheets and strips. The processes for making sheet metal have undergone a long series of improvements in the 20th century. As the methods were refined and made more economical, new uses for sheet metal were developed, and making sheet metal products became a well-established skilled craft field. Today, sheet metal workers are concerned with cutting, shaping, soldering, riveting, and other processes to fabricate, install, and maintain a wide range of articles. Heating, ventilating, and air-conditioning systems for all kinds of buildings—residential, commercial, industrial—provide the most important source of employment for sheet metal workers.

QUICK FACTS

School Subjects
Mathematics
Technical/shop

Personal Skills
Following instructions
Technical/scientific

Work Environment
Primarily indoors
One location with some
  travel

Minimum Education Level
Apprenticeship

Salary Range
$23,760 to $40,290 to
  $73,560

Certification or Licensing
None available

Outlook
More slowly than the average

DOT
804

GOE
06.02.02

NOC
7261

O*NET-SOC
47-2211.00

THE JOB

Most sheet metal workers handle a variety of tasks in fabricating, installing, and maintaining sheet metal products. Some workers concentrate on just one of these areas. Skilled workers must know about the whole range of activities involved in working with sheet metal.

Many sheet metal workers are employed by building contracting firms that construct or renovate residential, commercial, and industrial buildings. Fabricating and installing air-conditioning, heating, and refrigeration equipment is often a big part of their job. Some workers specialize in adjusting and servicing equipment that has already been installed so that it can operate at peak efficiency. Roofing contractors, the federal government, and businesses that do their own alteration and construction work also employ sheet metal workers. Other sheet metal workers are employed in the shipbuilding, railroad, and aircraft industries or in shops that manufacture specialty products such as custom kitchen equipment or electrical generating and distributing machinery.

Fabricating is often done in a shop away from the site where the product is to be installed. In fabricating products, workers usually begin by studying blueprints or drawings. After determining the amounts and kinds of materials required for the job, they make measurements and lay out the pattern on the appropriate pieces of metal. They may use measuring tapes and rulers and figure dimensions with the aid of calculators. Then, following the pattern they have marked on the metal, they cut out the sections with hand or power shears or other machine tools. They may shape the pieces with a hand or machine brake, which is a type of equipment used for bending and forming sheet metal, and punch or drill holes in the parts. As a last step before assembly, workers inspect the parts to verify that all of them are accurately shaped. Then they fasten the parts together by welding, soldering, bolting, riveting, cementing, or using special devices such as metal clips. After assembly, it may be necessary to smooth rough areas on the fabricated item with a file or grinding wheel.

Computers play an increasingly important role in several of these tasks. Computers help workers plan the layout efficiently, so that all the necessary sections can be cut from the metal stock while leaving the smallest possible amount of waste sheet metal. Computers also help guide saws, shears, and lasers that cut metal, as well as other machines that form the pieces into the desired shapes.

If the item has been fabricated in a shop, it is taken to the installation site. There, the sheet metal workers join together different sections of the final product. For example, they may connect sections of duct end to end. Some items, such as sections of duct, can be bought factory-made in standard sizes, and workers modify them at the installation site to meet the requirements of the situation. Once finished, duct work may be suspended with metal hangers from ceilings or attached to walls. Sometimes sheet metal workers weld, bolt, screw, or nail items into place. To complete the installation, they may need to make additional sheet metal parts or alter the items they have fabricated.

Some tasks in working with sheet metal, such as making metal roofing, are routinely done at the job site. Workers measure and cut sections of roof paneling, which interlock with grooving at the edges. They nail or weld the paneling to the roof deck to hold it in place and put metal molding over joints and around the edges, windows, and doors to finish off the roof.

REQUIREMENTS

High School

Requirements vary slightly, but applicants for sheet metal training programs must be high school graduates. High school courses that provide a good background are mechanical drawing, trigonometry, geometry, and shop classes.

Postsecondary Training

The best way to learn the skills necessary for working in this field is to complete an apprenticeship. Apprenticeships generally consist of a planned series of on-the-job work experiences plus classroom instruction in related subjects. The on-the-job training portion of apprenticeships, which last at least four years, includes about 8,000 hours of work. The classroom instruction totals approximately 600 hours, spread over the years of the apprenticeship. The training covers all aspects of sheet metal fabrication and installation.

Apprentices get practical experience in layout work, cutting, shaping, and installing sheet metal. They also learn to work with materials that may be used instead of metal, such as fiberglass and plastics. Under the supervision of skilled workers, they begin with simple tasks and gradually work up to the most complex. In the classroom, they learn blueprint reading, drafting, mathematics, computer operations, job safety, welding, and the principles of heating, air-conditioning, and ventilating systems.

Apprenticeships may be run by joint committees representing locals of the Sheet Metal Workers' International Association, an important union in the field, and local chapters of the Sheet Metal and Air Conditioning Contractors' National Association. Other apprenticeships are run by local chapters of a contractor group, the Associated Builders and Contractors.

A few sheet metal workers learn informally on the job while they are employed as helpers to experienced workers. They gradually develop skills when opportunities arise for learning. Like apprentices, helpers start out with simple jobs and in time take on more complicated work. However, the training that helpers get may not be as balanced as that for apprentices, and it may take longer for them to learn all that they need to know. Helpers often take vocational school courses to supplement their work experience.

Even after they have become experienced and well qualified in their field, sheet metal workers may need to take further training to keep their skills up to date. Such training is often sponsored by union groups or paid for by their employers.

Other Requirements

Sheet metal workers need to be in good physical condition, with good manual dexterity, hand-eye coordination, and the ability to visualize and understand shapes and forms. They should also like to solve problems, enjoy challenges, and be able to work as a member of a team.

EXPLORING

High school students can gauge their aptitude for and interest in some of the common activities of sheet metal workers by taking courses such as metal shop, blueprint reading, and mechanical drawing. A summer or part-time job as a helper with a contracting firm that does sheet metal work could provide an excellent opportunity to observe workers on the job. If such a job cannot be arranged, it may be possible to visit a construction site and perhaps to talk with a sheet metal worker who can give an insider's view of this job.

EMPLOYERS

Approximately 170,700 sheet metal workers are employed in the United States. About 63 percent of workers are employed in the construction industry. Most workers in this field are employed by sheet metal contractors; some workers with a great deal of experience go into business for themselves. Many sheet metal workers are members of the Sheet Metal and Air Conditioning Contractors' National Association.

STARTING OUT

People who would like to enter an apprentice program in this field can seek information about apprenticeships from local employers of sheet metal workers, such as sheet metal contractors or heating, air-conditioning, and refrigeration contractors; from the local office of the Sheet Metal and Air Conditioning Contractors' National Asso-

Objects Created by Sheet Metal Workers

- Air-conditioning, heating, and refrigeration equipment
- Airplane wings
- Building facades
- Car bodies
- Decorative items such as the New Year's Eve ball in Times Square
- Ductwork
- Medical tables and storage units
- Ship parts
- Signs
- Steel sheets
- Tubing
- Vehicle parts

Source: International Training Institute for the Sheet Metal and Air Conditioning Industry

ciation; or from the local sheet metal apprentice training office, the joint union-management apprenticeship committee. Information on apprenticeship programs also can be obtained from the local office of the state employment service or the state apprenticeship agency.

People who would rather enter this field as on-the-job trainees can contact contractors directly about jobs as helpers. Leads for specific jobs may be located through the state employment service or newspaper classified ads. Graduates of vocational or technical training programs may get assistance from the career services office at their schools.

ADVANCEMENT

Skilled and experienced sheet metal workers who work for contractors may be promoted to positions as supervisors and eventually job superintendents. Those who develop their skills through further training may move into related fields, such as welding. Some sheet metal workers become specialists in particular activities, such as design and layout work or estimating costs of installations. Some workers eventually go into business for themselves as independent sheet metal contractors.

EARNINGS

Sheet metal workers earned an average hourly wage of $19.37 in 2008, according to the U.S. Department of Labor. Overall, hourly earnings ranged from less than $11.43 to more than $35.63. Earnings vary in different parts of the country and tend to be highest in industrialized urban areas. Earnings also vary by industry, with the construction industry paying sheet metal workers the highest hourly rates. Apprentices begin at about 40 to 50 percent of the rate paid to experienced workers and receive periodic pay increases throughout their training. Some workers who are union members are eligible for supplemental pay from their union during periods of unemployment or when they are working less than full time.

Benefits for sheet metal workers depend on the employer; however, they usually include such items as health insurance and paid vacation days.

WORK ENVIRONMENT

Most sheet metal workers have a regular 40-hour workweek and receive extra pay for overtime. Most of their work is performed indoors, so they are less likely to lose wages due to bad weather than many other craftworkers involved in construction projects. Some work is done outdoors, occasionally in uncomfortably hot or cold conditions.

Workers sometimes have to work high above the ground, as when they install gutters and roofs, and sometimes in awkward, cramped positions, as when they install ventilation systems in buildings. Workers may have to be on their feet for long periods, and they may have to lift heavy objects. Possible hazards of the trade include cuts and burns from machinery and equipment, as well as falls from ladders and scaffolding. Workers must follow safety guidelines to avoid injuries and sometimes wear protective gear such as safety glasses. Sheet metal fabrication shops are usually well ventilated and properly heated and lighted, but at times they are quite noisy.

OUTLOOK

The U.S. Department of Labor predicts that employment for sheet metal workers will grow more slowly than the average for all occupations through 2016. Opportunities will be strongest for those who have completed an apprenticeship program and who have welding certification. Any growth in employment will be related to several factors. Many new residential, commercial, and industrial buildings will be constructed, requiring the skills of sheet metal workers, and many older buildings will need to have new energy-efficient heating, cooling, and ventilating systems installed in place of outdated systems. Existing equipment will need routine maintenance and repair. Decorative sheet metal products are becoming more popular for some uses, a trend that is expected to provide an increasing amount of employment for sheet metal workers. Still, most of the demand for new workers in this field will be to replace experienced people who are transferring to other jobs or leaving the workforce altogether.

Job prospects will vary somewhat with economic conditions. In general, the economy is closely tied to the level of new building construction activity. During economic downturns, workers may face periods of unemployment, while at other times there may be more jobs than skilled workers available to take them. But overall, sheet metal workers are less affected by economic ups and downs than some other craftworkers in the construction field. This is because activities related to maintenance, repair, and replacement of old equipment compose a significant part of their job, and even during an economic slump, building owners are often inclined to go ahead with such work.

FOR MORE INFORMATION

For information on state apprenticeship programs, visit
Employment & Training Administration
U.S. Department of Labor
http://www.doleta.gov

For industry and career information, contact the following organizations:
International Training Institute for the Sheet Metal and Air Conditioning Industry
601 North Fairfax Street, Suite 240
Alexandria, VA 22314-2083
Tel: 703-739-7200
http://www.sheetmetal-iti.org

Sheet Metal and Air Conditioning Contractors' National Association
4201 Lafayette Center Drive
Chantilly, VA 20151-1209
Tel: 703-803-2980
Email: info@smacna.org
http://www.smacna.org

Sheet Metal Workers International Association
1750 New York Avenue, NW, 6th Floor
Washington, DC 20006-5301
Tel: 202-783-5880
http://www.smwia.org

Surveyors

OVERVIEW

Surveyors mark exact measurements and locations of elevations, points, lines, and contours on or near the earth's surface. They measure distances between points to determine property boundaries and to provide data for mapmaking, construction projects, and other engineering purposes. There are approximately 57,600 surveyors employed in the United States.

HISTORY

As the United States expanded from the Atlantic to the Pacific, people moved over the mountains and plains into the uncharted regions of the West. They found it necessary to chart their routes and to mark property lines and borderlines by surveying and filing claims.

The need for accurate geographical measurements and precise records of those measurements has increased over the years. Surveying measurements are needed to determine the location of a trail, highway, or road; the site of a log cabin, frame house, or skyscraper; the right-of-way for water pipes, drainage ditches, and telephone lines; and for the charting of unexplored regions, bodies of water, land, and underground mines.

QUICK FACTS

School Subjects
Geography
Mathematics

Personal Skills
Communication/ideas
Technical/scientific

Work Environment
Primarily outdoors
Primarily multiple locations

Minimum Education Level
Some postsecondary training

Salary Range
$29,600 to $52,980 to
$85,620+

Certification or Licensing
Required

Outlook
Faster than the average

DOT
018

GOE
02.08.01

NOC
2154

O*NET-SOC
17-1022.00

As a result, the demand for professional surveyors has grown and become more complex. New computerized systems (such as Geographic Information Systems and light-imaging detection and ranging technology) are now used to map, store, and retrieve geographical data more accurately and efficiently. This new technology has not only improved the process of surveying but extended its reach as well. Surveyors can now make detailed maps of ocean floors and the moon's surface.

THE JOB

On proposed construction projects, such as highways, airstrips, and housing developments, it is the surveyor's responsibility to make necessary measurements through an accurate and detailed survey of the area. The surveyor usually works with a field party consisting of several people. Instrument assistants, called *surveying and mapping technicians*, handle a variety of surveying instruments including the theodolite, transit, level, surveyor's chain, rod, and other electronic equipment. In the course of the survey, it is important that all readings be recorded accurately and field notes maintained so that the survey can be checked for accuracy.

Surveyors may specialize in one or more particular types of surveying.

Land surveyors establish township, property, and other tract-of-land boundary lines. Using maps, notes, or actual land title deeds, they survey the land, checking for the accuracy of existing records. This information is used to prepare legal documents such as deeds and leases. *Land surveying managers* coordinate the work of surveyors, their parties, and legal, engineering, architectural, and other staff involved in a project. These managers also develop policy, prepare budgets, certify work upon completion, and handle numerous other administrative duties.

Highway surveyors establish grades, lines, and other points of reference for highway construction projects. This survey information is essential to the work of the numerous engineers and the construction crews who build the new highway.

Geodetic surveyors measure large masses of land, sea, and space that must take into account the curvature of Earth and its geophysical characteristics. Their work is helpful in establishing points of reference for smaller land surveys, determining national boundaries, and preparing maps. *Geodetic computers* calculate latitude, longitude, angles, areas, and other information needed for mapmaking. They work from field notes made by an engineering survey party and also use reference tables and a calculating machine or computer.

Marine surveyors measure harbors, rivers, and other bodies of water. They determine the depth of the water by measuring sound waves in relation to nearby land masses. Their work is essential for planning and constructing navigation projects, such as breakwaters, dams, piers, marinas, and bridges, and for preparing nautical charts and maps.

Mine surveyors make surface and underground surveys, preparing maps of mines and mining operations. Such maps are helpful in examining underground passages within the levels of a mine and assessing the volume and location of raw material available.

Geophysical prospecting surveyors locate and mark sites considered likely to contain petroleum deposits. *Oil-well directional surveyors* use sonic, electronic, and nuclear measuring instruments to gauge the presence and amount of oil- and gas-bearing reservoirs. *Pipeline surveyors* determine rights-of-way for oil construction projects, providing information essential to the preparation for and laying of the lines.

Photogrammetric engineers determine the contour of an area to show elevations and depressions and indicate such features as mountains, lakes, rivers, forests, roads, farms, buildings, and other landmarks. Aerial, land, and water photographs are taken with special equipment able to capture images of very large areas. From these pictures, accurate measurements of the terrain and surface features can be made. These surveys are helpful in construction projects and in the preparation of topographical maps. Photogrammetry is particularly helpful in charting areas that are inaccessible or difficult to travel.

Forensic surveyors serve as expert witnesses in legal proceedings that involve industrial, automobile, or other types of accidents. They gather, analyze, and map data that is used as evidence at a trial, hearing, or lawsuit. These professionals must have extensive experience in the field and be strong communicators in order to explain technical information to people who do not have a background in surveying.

REQUIREMENTS

High School

To prepare for a career as a surveyor, take plenty of math and science courses in high school. Take algebra, geometry, and trigonometry to become comfortable making different calculations. Earth science, chemistry, and physics classes should also be helpful. Geography will help you learn about different locations, their characteristics, and cartography. Benefits from taking mechanical drawing and other drafting classes include an increased ability to visualize abstractions, exposure to detailed work, and an understanding of perspectives. Taking computer science classes will prepare you for working with technical surveying equipment.

Postsecondary Training
Depending on state requirements, you will need some postsecondary education. The quickest route is by earning a bachelor's degree in surveying or engineering combined with on-the-job training. Other entry options include obtaining more job experience combined with a one- to three-year program in surveying and surveying technology offered by community colleges, technical institutes, and vocational schools.

Certification or Licensing
The American Congress on Surveying and Mapping (ACSM) has partnered with the Federal Emergency Management Agency to create a certification program for floodplain surveyors. Contact the ACSM for details on the program.

All 50 states require that surveyors making property and boundary surveys be licensed or registered. The requirements for licensure vary, but most require a degree in surveying or a related field, a certain number of years of experience, and passing of examinations in land surveying (typically a written examination given by the National Council of Examiners for Engineering and Surveying). Generally, the higher the degree obtained, the less experience required. Those with bachelor's degrees may need only two to four years of on-the-job experience, while those with a lesser degree may need up to 12 years of prior experience to obtain a license. Information on specific requirements can be obtained by contacting the licensure department of the state in which you plan to work. If you are seeking employment in the federal government, you must take a civil service examination and meet the educational, experience, and other specified requirements for the position.

Other Requirements
The ability to work with numbers and perform mathematical computations accurately and quickly is very important. Other helpful qualities are the ability to visualize and understand objects in two and three dimensions (spatial relationships) and the ability to discriminate between and compare shapes, sizes, lines, shadings, and other forms (form perception).

Surveyors walk a great deal and carry equipment over all types of terrain, so endurance and coordination are important physical assets. In addition, surveyors direct and supervise the work of their team, so you should be good at working with other people and demonstrate leadership abilities.

EXPLORING

While you are in high school, begin to familiarize yourself with terms, projects, and tools used in this profession by reading books and magazines on the topic, such as *Professional Surveyor Magazine* (http://www.profsurv.com). One of the best opportunities for experience is a summer job with a construction firm or company that requires survey work. Even if the job does not involve direct contact with survey crews, it will offer an opportunity to observe surveyors and talk with them about their work. Additionally, you should visit http://www.surveying career.com for more information on career opportunities in the field.

Some colleges have work-study programs that offer on-the-job experience. These opportunities, like summer or part-time jobs, provide helpful contacts in the field that may lead to future full-time employment. If your college does not offer a work-study program and you can't find a paying summer job, consider volunteering at an appropriate government agency. The U.S. Geological Survey and the Bureau of Land Management usually offer volunteer opportunities in select areas.

EMPLOYERS

Approximately 57,600 surveyors are employed in the United States. According to the U.S. Department of Labor, almost 70 percent of surveying workers in the United States are employed by engineering, architectural, and surveying firms. Local, state, and federal (mainly the U.S. Geological Society, the Bureau of Land Managemet, the U.S. Forest Service, the National Oceanic and Atmospheric Administration, and the Army Corps of Engineers) agencies are the next largest employers of surveying workers, and the majority of the remaining surveyors work for construction firms, oil and gas extraction companies, and public utilities. Only a small number of surveyors are self-employed.

STARTING OUT

Apprentices with a high school education can enter the field as equipment operators or surveying assistants. Those who have postsecondary education can enter the field more easily, beginning as surveying and mapping technicians.

College graduates can learn about job openings through their schools' career services offices or through potential employers that may visit their campus. Many cities have employment agencies that specialize in seeking out workers for positions in surveying and related fields. Check your local newspaper or telephone book or look online to see if such recruiting firms exist in your area.

ADVANCEMENT

With experience, workers advance through the leadership ranks within a surveying team. Workers begin as assistants and then can move into positions such as senior technician, party chief, and, finally, licensed surveyor. Because surveying work is closely related to other fields, surveyors can move into electrical, mechanical, or chemical engineering or specialize in drafting.

EARNINGS

In 2008 surveyors earned a median annual salary of $52,980. According to the U.S. Department of Labor, the middle 50 percent earned between $38,800 and $70,010 a year. The lowest paid 10 percent earned less than $29,600, and the highest paid 10 percent earned more than $85,620 a year. In general, the federal government paid the highest wages to its surveyors, $78,710 a year in 2008.

Most positions with the federal, state, and local governments and with private firms provide life and medical insurance, pension, vacation, and holiday benefits.

WORK ENVIRONMENT

Surveyors work 40-hour weeks except when overtime is necessary to meet a project deadline. The peak work period is during the summer months when weather conditions are most favorable. However, it is not uncommon for the surveyor to be exposed to adverse weather conditions.

Some survey projects may involve hazardous conditions, depending on the region and climate as well as the plant and animal life. Survey crews may encounter snakes, poison ivy, and other hazardous plant and animal life, and may suffer heat exhaustion, sunburn, and frostbite while in the field. Survey projects, particularly those near construction projects or busy highways, may impose dangers of injury from heavy traffic, flying objects, and other accidental hazards. Unless the surveyor is employed only for office assignments, the work location most likely will change from survey to survey.

Some assignments may require the surveyor to be away from home for periods of time.

OUTLOOK

The U.S. Department of Labor predicts that employment of surveyors will grow faster than the average for all occupations through 2018 as a result of the widespread use of technology such as the Global Positioning System and Geographic Information Systems, and the increasing demand for detailed geographic information. The outlook will be best for surveyors who have college degrees, advanced field experience, and strong technical and computer skills.

Growth in urban and suburban areas (with the need for new streets, homes, shopping centers, schools, and gas and water lines) will provide employment opportunities. State and federal highway improvement programs and local urban redevelopment programs also will provide jobs for surveyors. The expansion of industrial and business firms and the relocation of some firms to large undeveloped tracts will also create job openings. However, construction projects are closely tied to the state of the economy, so employment may fluctuate from year to year.

FOR MORE INFORMATION

For more information on accredited surveying programs, contact
Accreditation Board for Engineering and Technology
111 Market Place, Suite 1050
Baltimore, MD 21202-4012
Tel: 410-347-7700
http://www.abet.org

For information on geodetic surveying, contact
American Association for Geodetic Surveying
Six Montgomery Village Avenue, Suite 403
Gaithersburg, MD 20879-3546
Tel: 240-632-8943
http://www.aagsmo.org

For information on certification and state affiliates and colleges and universities that offer land surveying programs, contact
American Congress on Surveying and Mapping
Six Montgomery Village Avenue, Suite 403
Gaithersburg, MD 20879-3546

Tel: 240-632-9716
http://www.acsm.net

For information on photogrammetry and careers in the field, contact
American Society for Photogrammetry and Remote Sensing
5410 Grosvenor Lane, Suite 210
Bethesda, MD 20814-2160
Tel: 301-493-0290
Email: asprs@asprs.org
http://www.asprs.org

For information on volunteer and employment opportunities with the federal government, contact
Bureau of Land Management
Office of Public Affairs
1849 C Street, Room 406-LS
Washington, DC 20240-0001
Tel: 202-208-3801
http://www.blm.gov

U.S. Geological Survey
12201 Sunrise Valley Drive
Reston, VA 20192-0002
Tel: 888-275-8747
http://www.usgs.gov

For more information on Geographic Information Systems (GIS), visit
GIS.com
http://www.gis.com

For comprehensive information on careers in surveying, visit
Measuring the World Around Us: A High-Tech Career In Professional Surveying
http://www.surveyingcareer.com

For information on certification, contact
National Society of Professional Surveyors
Six Montgomery Village Avenue, Suite 403
Gaithersburg, MD 20879-3557
Tel: 240-632-9716
http://www.nspsmo.org

Welders

OVERVIEW

Welders operate a variety of special equipment to join metal parts together permanently, usually using heat and sometimes pressure. They work on constructing and repairing automobiles, aircraft, ships, buildings, bridges, highways, appliances, and many other metal structures and manufactured products.

HISTORY

Although some welding techniques were used more than 1,000 years ago in forging iron blades by hand, modern welding processes were first employed in the latter half of the 1800s. From experimental beginnings, the pioneers in this field developed a wide variety of innovative processes. These included resistance welding, invented in 1877, in which an electric current is sent through metal parts in contact. Electrical resistance and pressure melt the metal at the area of contact. Gas welding, also developed in the same era, is a relatively simple process of using a torch that burns a gas such as acetylene to create enough heat to melt and fuse metal parts. Oxyacetylene welding, a version of this process developed a few years later, is a common welding process still used today. Arc welding, first used commercially in 1889, relies on an electric arc to generate heat. Thermite welding, which fuses metal pieces with the intense heat of a chemical reaction, was first used around 1900.

In the last century, the sudden demand for vehicles and armaments and a growing list of industrial uses for welding that resulted from the two world wars have spurred researchers to keep improving welding processes and also have encouraged the development of numerous new processes. Today, there are more than 80 different types of welding and welding-related processes. Some of the newer processes include laser-beam welding and electron-beam welding. Automated welding, in which a robot or machine completes a welding task while being monitored by a welder, welding technician, or machine operator, is becoming an increasingly popular production method. This development is not expected to greatly affect the employment of welders, however, since the machinery must be operated by someone who has knowledge of welding to ensure that a proper weld has been made.

THE JOB

Welders use various kinds of equipment and processes to create the heat and pressure needed to melt the edges of metal pieces in a controlled fashion so that the pieces may be joined permanently. The processes can be grouped into three categories. The arc welding process derives heat from an electric arc between two electrodes or between an electrode and the workpiece. The gas welding process produces heat by burning a mixture of oxygen and some other combustible gas, such as acetylene or hydrogen. The resistance welding process obtains heat from pressure and resistance by the workpiece to an electric current. Two of these processes, the arc and gas methods, can also be used to cut, gouge, or finish metal.

Depending on which of these processes and equipment they use, welders may be designated *arc welders, gas welders,* or *acetylene welders*; *combination welders* (meaning they use a combination of gas and arc welding); or *welding machine operators* (meaning they operate machines that use an arc welding process, electron-beam welding process, laser-beam welding process, or friction welding process). Other workers in the welding field include *resistance machine welders; oxygen cutters,* who use gas torches to cut or trim metals; and *arc cutters,* who use an electric arc to cut or trim metals.

Skilled welders usually begin by planning and laying out their work based on drawings, blueprints, or other specifications. Using their working knowledge of the properties of the metal, they determine the proper sequence of operations needed for the job. They may work with steel, stainless steel, cast iron, bronze, aluminum, nickel, and other metals and alloys. Metal pieces to be welded may be in a variety of positions, such as flat, vertical, horizontal, or overhead.

In the manual arc welding process (the most commonly used), welders grasp a holder containing a suitable electrode and adjust the electric current supplied to the electrode. Then they strike an arc (an electric discharge across a gap) by touching the electrode to the metal. Next, they guide the electrode along the metal seam to be welded, allowing sufficient time for the heat of the arc to melt the metal. The molten metal from the electrode is deposited in the joint and, together with the molten metal edges of the base metal, solidifies to form a solid connection. Welders determine the correct kind of electrode to use based on the job specifications and their knowledge of the materials.

In gas welding, welders melt the metal edges with an intensely hot flame from the combustion of fuel gases in welding torches. First, they obtain the proper types of torch tips and welding rods, which are rods of a filler metal that goes into the weld seam. They adjust the regulators on the tanks of fuel gases, such as oxygen and acetylene, and they light the torch. To obtain the proper size and quality of flame, welders adjust the gas valves on the torch and hold the flame against the metal until it is hot enough. Then they apply the welding rod to the molten metal to supply the extra filler needed to complete the weld.

Maintenance welders, another category of welding workers, may use any of the various welding techniques. They travel to construction sites, utility installations, and other locations to make on-site repairs to metalwork.

Some workers in the welding field do repetitive production tasks using automatic welding equipment. In general, automatic welding is not used where there are critical safety and strength requirements. The surfaces that these welders work on are usually in only one position. Resistance machine welders often work in the mass production of parts, doing the same welding operations repeatedly. To operate the welding machine, they first make adjustments to control the electric current and pressure and then feed in and align the workpieces. After completing the welding operation, welders remove the work from the machine. Welders must constantly monitor the process in order to make sure that the machine is producing the proper weld.

To cut metal, oxygen cutters may use hand-guided torches or machine-mounted torches. They direct the flame of burning oxygen and fuel gas onto the area to be cut until it melts. Then, an additional stream of gas is released from the torch, which cuts the metal along previously marked lines. Arc cutters follow a similar procedure in their work, except that they use an electric arc as the source of heat. As in oxygen cutting, an additional stream of gas may be released when cutting the metal.

REQUIREMENTS

High School

High school graduates are preferred for trainee positions for skilled jobs. Useful high school courses for prospective welders include mathematics, blueprint reading, mechanical drawing, applied physics, and shop. If possible, the shop courses should cover the basics of welding and working with electricity.

Postsecondary Training

Many welders learn their skills in formal training programs in welding, such as those available in many community colleges, technical institutes, trade schools, and the armed forces. Some programs are short term and narrow in focus, while others provide several years of thorough preparation for a variety of jobs.

A high school diploma or its equivalent is required for admission into these programs. Beginners can also learn welding skills in on-the-job training programs. The length of such training programs ranges from several days or weeks for jobs requiring few skills to a period of one to three years for skilled jobs. Trainees often begin as helpers to experienced workers, doing very simple tasks. As they learn, they are given more challenging work. To learn some skilled jobs, trainees supplement their on-the-job training with formal classroom instruction in technical aspects of the trade.

Various programs sponsored by federal, state, and local governments provide training opportunities in some areas. These training programs, which usually stress the fundamentals of welding, may be in the classroom or on the job and last from a few weeks to a year. Apprenticeship programs also offer training. Apprenticeships that teach a range of metalworking skills, including the basics of welding, are run by trade unions such as the International Association of Machinists and Aerospace Workers.

Certification or Licensing

To do welding work where the strength of the weld is a critical factor (such as in aircraft, bridges, boilers, or high-pressure pipelines), welders may have to pass employer tests or standardized examinations for certification by government agencies or professional and technical associations (such as the American Welding Society).

Other Requirements

Employers generally prefer to hire applicants who are in good enough physical condition to bend, stoop, and work in awkward positions.

Applicants also need manual dexterity, good hand-eye coordination, and good eyesight, as well as patience and the ability to concentrate for extended periods as they work on a task.

Many people in welding and related occupations belong to one of the following unions: the International Association of Machinists and Aerospace Workers; the International Brotherhood of Boilermakers, Iron Ship Builders, Blacksmiths, Forgers and Helpers; the International Union, United Automobile, Aerospace and Agricultural Implement Workers of America; the United Association of Journeymen and Apprentices of the Plumbing and Pipe Fitting Industry of the United States and Canada; or the United Electrical, Radio, and Machine Workers of America.

EXPLORING

With the help of a teacher or a guidance counselor, students may be able to arrange to visit a workplace where they can observe welders or welding machine operators on the job. Ideally, such a visit can provide a chance to see several welding processes and various kinds of welding work and working conditions, as well as an opportunity to talk with welders about their work.

EMPLOYERS

Workers in welding occupations work in a variety of settings. About two-thirds of welders are employed in manufacturing plants that produce motor vehicles, ships, boilers, machinery, appliances, and other metal products. Other welders work for repair shops or construction companies that build bridges, large buildings, pipelines, and similar metal structures. All welding machine operators work in manufacturing industries.

STARTING OUT

Graduates of good training programs in welding often receive help in finding jobs through their schools' career services offices. The classified ads sections of newspapers often carry listings of local job openings. Information about openings for trainee positions, apprenticeships, and government training programs, as well as jobs for skilled workers, may be available through the local offices of an individual's state employment service and local offices of unions that organize welding workers. Job seekers also can apply directly to the personnel offices at companies that hire welders.

ADVANCEMENT

Advancement usually depends on acquiring additional skills. Workers who gain experience and learn new processes and techniques are increasingly valuable to their employers, and they may be promoted to positions as supervisors, inspectors, or welding instructors. With further formal technical training, welders may qualify for welding technician jobs. Some experienced welders go into business for themselves and open their own welding and repair shops.

EARNINGS

The earnings of welding trades workers vary widely depending on the skills needed for the job, industry, location, and other factors. The U.S. Department of Labor reports that median annual earnings of welders in 2008 were $33,560. On average, welders and welding machine operators can expect annual earnings in the range of $22,570 to $50,700 or more. In addition to wages, employers often provide fringe benefits, such as health insurance plans, paid vacation time, paid sick time, and pension plans.

WORK ENVIRONMENT

Welders may spend their workday inside well-ventilated and well-lighted shops and factories, outside at a construction site, or in confined spaces, such as in an underground tunnel or inside a large storage tank that is being built. Welding jobs can involve working in uncomfortable positions. Sometimes welders work for short periods in booths that are built to contain sparks and glare. In some jobs, workers must repeat the same procedure over and over.

Welders often encounter hazardous conditions and may need to wear goggles, helmets with protective faceplates, protective clothing, safety shoes, and other gear to prevent burns and other injuries. Many metals give off toxic gases and fumes when heated, and workers must be careful to avoid exposure to such harmful substances. Other potential dangers include electric shock and explosions from mishandling combustible gases. Workers in this field must learn the safest ways of carrying out welding work and always pay attention to safety procedures. Various trade and safety organizations have developed rules for welding procedures, safety practices, and health precautions that can minimize the risks of the job. Operators of automatic welding machines are exposed to fewer hazards than manual welders and cutters, and they usually need to use less protective gear.

Fifty percent of welders work 40 hours a week, although overtime is common. In fact, 20 percent of welders work 50 or more hours per week. Welders may work shifts of up to 12 hours in length.

OUTLOOK

Overall employment in welding and related occupations is expected to experience little or no change through 2018, according to the U.S. Department of Labor. Despite this prediction, opportunities are expected to be excellent for well-trained welders. There should be plenty of jobs for welders because many employers have difficulties finding qualified applicants. Most job openings will develop when experienced workers leave their jobs. However, the outlook varies somewhat by industry. In manufacturing industries, the trend toward increasing automation, including more use of welding robots, is expected to decrease the demand for manual welders and increase the demand for welding machine operators. In construction, wholesale trade and in repair services, more skilled welders will be needed as the economy grows because the work tends to be less routine in these industries, and automation is not likely to be a big factor. During periods when the economy is in a slowdown, many workers in construction and manufacturing, including some welders, may be laid off.

FOR MORE INFORMATION

For information on welding careers, scholarships, certification, and a free DVD and career brochure, contact
American Welding Society
550 NW LeJeune Road
Miami, FL 33126-5649
Tel: 800-443-9353
Email: info@aws.org
http://www.aws.org and http://awssection.org/index.php/forms/
   career_guide

For information on state apprenticeship programs, visit
Employment & Training Administration
U.S. Department of Labor
http://www.doleta.gov

For information on union membership, contact
International Association of Machinists and Aerospace Workers
9000 Machinists Place
Upper Marlboro, MD 20772-2687
Tel: 301-967-4500
http://www.goiam.org

══════════════════ INTERVIEW ══════════════════

Joe Dusek is the coordinator of the welding and fabrication program at Triton College in River Grove, Illinois. He discussed the field with the editors of Careers in Focus: Construction.

Q. Can you tell us about your program?

A. Triton College offers a Metal Inert Gas (MIG) & Tungsten Inert Gas (TIG) welding certificate that consists of four basic, four-semester hour courses. [Both MIG and TIG welding are subspecialties of arc welding.] The 16-credit program lasts two years. The semesters break down as follows: Semester One: Fundamentals of Welding; Semester Two: Welding & Fabrication Techniques; Semester Three: Advanced Welding I; and Semester Four: Advanced Welding Techniques. This certificate prepares students for the American Welding Society (AWS) certification exam.

Q. What is one thing that young people may not know about a career in welding?

A. Remember that welders are craftsmen; like any other trade the quality of their work reflects on them. The work can be tedious, but rewarding. I'd even say that welders must have a certain artistic sense to do what they do. Each project is unique, requiring a specific weld type or material. Many welders create metal sculptures in their spare time.

Q. What advice would you offer welding students as they graduate and look for jobs?

A. Most importantly, they must be AWS certified. This shows any employer that the welder has passed an intense skills test.

Q. What is the employment outlook for the field?

A. Most of our students find employment after taking the first class. They earn their certificate to take the AWS exam and advance their careers. Welding remains a job with skills that are in high demand. Most people tend to overlook it as a career choice, thus there's a shortage of welders. A welder will always find work.

Additional Careers

The following careers represent other opportunities in the construction industry:

Construction laborers do a variety of tasks at the construction sites of buildings, highways, bridges, and other public and private building projects. Depending on the type of project, construction laborers may carry materials used by craft workers, clean up debris, operate cement mixers, or lay and seal together lengths of sewer pipe, among other duties. They also are involved in hazardous waste/environmental remediation.

Elevator installers and repairers, also called *elevator constructors* or *elevator mechanics,* are skilled crafts workers who assemble, install, and repair elevators, escalators, dumbwaiters, and similar equipment. They may also modernize this equipment when possible.

Glaziers select, cut, fit, and install all types of glass and glass substitutes such as plastics. They install windows, mirrors, shower doors, glass tabletops, display cases, skylights, special items such as preassembled stained glass and leaded glass window panels, and many other glass items.

Insulation workers install building materials called insulation, which keeps hot or cold air in or out of a space. Office buildings, homes, trucks, steam pipes, attics, and boiler rooms all need insulation to stay at the proper temperature and to ensure proper heating and cooling.

Ironworkers fabricate, assemble, and install structural and reinforcing metal products used in the construction of buildings and bridges. They also install steel walls, iron stairways, and other metal components of buildings; assemble large metal tanks for chemicals, water, and oil; and do similar structural work with other metals.

Lathers work with lath, a supporting base made out of metal, plastic, or gypsum, which is fastened to walls, ceilings, and roofs. Lath provides a foundation for the application of plaster, tile, roofing material, fireproofing, and acoustical material. (Lathers should not be confused with machinists who work on power-driven equipment called lathes.)

Road crew workers help to maintain and repair the roadways, which include country roads, freeways, bike paths, and runways. They also build new roads, repave old roads, clear snow and ice, and cut the grass at the side of highways.

Surveying and mapping technicians help determine, describe, and record geographic areas or features. They are usually the leading assistant to the professional surveyor, civil engineer, and map-maker. They operate modern surveying and mapping instruments and may participate in other operations. Technicians must have a basic knowledge of the current practices and legal implications of surveys to establish and record property size, shape, topography, and boundaries. They often supervise other assistants during routine surveying conducted within the bounds established by a professional surveyor.

Welding technicians are the link between the welder and the engineer and work to improve a wide variety of welding processes. As part of their duties, they may supervise, inspect, and find applications for the welding processes. Some technicians work in research facilities, where they help engineers test and evaluate newly developed welding equipment, metals, and alloys. When new equipment is being developed or old equipment improved, they conduct experiments on it, evaluate the data, and then make recommendations to engineers. Other welding technicians, who work in the field, inspect welded joints and conduct tests to ensure that welds meet company standards, national code requirements, and customer job specifications.

Index

Entries and page numbers in **bold** indicate major treatment of a topic.

P